Contents

I Have a Voice
How to Stop Stuttering

Bob G. Bodenhamer, DMin

Edited by Peter Young
Foreword to the paperback edition by
L. Michael Hall

Foreword by John C. Harrison

Crown House Publishing Limited
www.crownhouse.co.uk
www.crownhousepublishing.com

First published by

Crown House Publishing Ltd
Crown Buildings, Bancyfelin, Carmarthen, Wales, SA33 5ND, UK
www.crownhouse.co.uk

and

Crown House Publishing Company LLC
6 Trowbridge Drive, Suite 5, Bethel CT 06801-2858, USA
www.crownhousepublishing.com

Originally published in hardback as *Mastering Blocking and Stuttering*
(ISBN: 1904424406)

"Neuro-semantics" and "Meta-states" are registered trademarks of
the Institute of Neuro-Semantics

British Library Cataloguing-in-Publication Data
A catalogue entry for this book is available
from the British Library.

13 digit ISBN 978-184590727-3
10 digit ISBN 1845907272

LCCN 2011926832

Printed and bound in the USA

Foreword to the paperback edition

by Bob G. Bodenhamer and L. Michael Hall

Stuttering is in the shadows of public awareness and has been for years. But no more! Now there is a movie that is bringing it forth front and center. Sure, no one dies from stuttering, and it is not pervasive: only one percent of people stutter. Yet it is a malady that has not received a great deal of attention.

But no longer is it in the shadows. In November 2010, a movie brought stuttering to the world's attention. *The King's Speech*, a British historical drama directed by Tom Hooper and written by David Seidler made stuttering part of the public conversation. Moviegoers learned of the embarrassing pain that most People Who Stutter (PWS) suffer. But, even more than that, Lionel Logue, the speech trainer in the movie, brings into focus this shocking fact: stuttering is not about speech! It is about the "thinking" that is mostly unconscious and in "the back of the mind" of the PWS.

Positioned in the 1930s, the movie is about the young man who became the King of England just prior to the Second World War. It reveals the painful experiences that stuttering created for him. Logue, an Australian, who became the King's speech trainer, used techniques to enable the King to gain more control of his stuttering in ways that were quite advanced for that time. Many things in this movie give support to the theories that you will find in the pages of this book.

So what did Logue do? Mainly and primarily he challenged the mental frames that created the stuttering. He knew that stuttering was not a problem of flawed neurology or genetics. He knew that it was a problem of the person's attitudes and beliefs (mental frames) about stuttering. To create a good case of stuttering, there are certain belief frames a person has to adopt. The person has to believe such things as:

- Mis-speaking is a terrible, horrible, and awful experience.

- Mis-speaking means "I'm inadequate as a person."

- Mis-speaking means "No one will like me, want to be around me, value me, love me. They will laugh at me and reject me."

- Mis-speaking means "I have to stop myself from stuttering and pay attention to each and every word that comes out of my mouth."

- Mis-speaking means "It's impossible. I can't stop it. Trying to stop it only makes it worse. I must indeed be inadequate as a human being."

- Mis-speaking means "I cannot have a career nor can I ever marry – who would want to marry me?"

Mis-speaking is terrifying because of the meanings given to it. It is the meanings given to stuttering that this book addresses. *The King's Speech* serves as a support for the radical views contained within this work. Indeed, we believe that stuttering is a phobia of mis-speaking, with the painful feelings being located in the throat and other muscles that are involved in speaking. If you do not believe this, look up the diagnosis of a panic attack in the DSM-IV[1]. Does the description of a panic attack not describe exactly what you experience when you are having a speech block?

Logue knew this as he so passionately tries to get the King to understand that stuttering is about a specific behavior, speaking, and not about who he is. Logue as much says, "Bertie, your brain isn't broken. It is doing exactly what you instruct it to do. The problem is your mental frames about stuttering!" The mental frames listed above are the frames that create the problem. And that is why when you change those frames, the stuttering behavior changes.

In the movie, *The King's Speech*, you see Logue's actions as he assists Bertie, the King, in changing his mental frames. We have identified six key mental frames that were driving Bertie's stuttering:

1.   Demanding-ness – Logue challenges his frames about demanding-ness. "Bertie, call me Lionel; here we are equals." This changes the context (which changes meaning). Later he says, "Say it to me as a friend."

2.   Exceptions – We have found out that most every PWS has exceptions – places, times, and people – with whom and where they do not stutter. When do you not stutter? Do you stutter with your dog? Do you stutter when you are alone? Do you stutter when among trusted friends? In the movie, Logue asks, "Do you stutter when you think?" "No, of course not." Ah, so here's an exception! So you do know how to think or pray or talk to your dog without stuttering! So if there's an exception, what is the difference that makes a difference in that exception? If you develop that, you'll have developed a powerful first step to a resolution.

3.   Singing – In the movie, Logue asks Bertie to sing it. Find a tune that you know well and whatever it is that you are trying to say, sing it. "Let the sounds flow," Logue explains. This accepts the experience and changes one element in it. The King thinks it silly, ridiculous, and refuses to do it at first, but then he finds that he can move through the blocking by using a tune and putting the words to the tune. Singing creates both rhythm and air flow, both of which aid the PWS in speaking fluently.

4.   Judgmentalism – It takes Logue a long time, but eventually the King talks about being mercilessly teased about his mis-speaking as a young boy. He was teased by his brother who put him down and who judged him because he stuttered. Important to the creation of negative meaning frames, Bertie's father also judged him harshly without showing any mercy. This is deadly to the PWS. Logue comments:

"You don't need to be afraid of the things you were afraid of at five. You are your own man now."

What great frames! The past-is-the-past and what you feared as a five-year-old doesn't need to be fearful now as a man. You once were controlled by others, now you are your own person. Breaking these judgment frames is critical. PWS have to master the childish fear that others will judge them for failing to be fluent.

And yet, even more important, is that they will have to master their own self-judgments.

The movie portrays this in a fascinating way. It occurs when Logue invites the King to read a famous text. When he does so, because he can hear himself, he is simultaneously judging himself. But when Logue turns up some music and plays it so loudly the King cannot hear himself reading, he reads the literature fluently, only he does not recognize it. And because he is so impatient, so self-critical, so non-accepting of the process, he storms out. However, he takes with him the recording that Logue has made and at a later time, late at night, he puts on the record and listens. He is amazed! The recording only recorded his voice and not the loud music – and he was reading fluently. Why? What was the difference? When he could not hear himself, he was unable to judge himself.

5.   True to your own emotions – The movie portrays another process when Logue provokes the King to anger. He notices that when the King gets angry enough to curse, at that point he does not stutter. "Do you know the 'F' word?" he asks. At another time he "reproves" and "commands" him regarding sitting in a chair, "You can't sit there!" It frustrates and angers the King to be talked to that way by a commoner! Logue thus brings his ability to be fluent-while-cursing to his attention.

What's going on here? Bertie is frustrated and angry enough to curse – and when he curses, he is fluent! When he curses, he moves beyond the frame of caring what people may think should he stutter. Bertie is true to his emotions – to himself. This leads to fluency, because, generally speaking, PWS dismiss their emotions. Indeed, they believe that to give themselves permission to feel their emotions will result somehow in their being hurt. This belief is rooted in Bertie's childhood experiences with his brother and his father.

6.   Focusing elsewhere – Finally there is the scene where Logue brings Bertie into his home. There is a model plane on the table in the process of being put together. When the King was a child he was not allowed to play with model planes, so Logue encourages him to play with it. As he becomes preoccupied and focuses on the plane, his speech gets more and more fluent. Ah, again, this is an

experience that moves him outside of his usual frames of judgment, of disapproval, and of over-consciousness of speaking.

Due to his lack of knowledge of the yet-to-be-discovered field of cognitive psychology, Logue was limited in what he could do to help the King. The book you now have in your hand is filled with suggestions and patterns that will assist you in changing those negative meanings that have been driving your stuttering. Remember, as with the King, when you change the meanings about stuttering, the speaking changes. And that's the potential we wish for you to unleash!

Notes:

1 *Diagnostic and Statistical Manual of Mental Disorders, Fourth Edition* (DSM-IV). (2000). Washington, DC: American Psychological Association.

Our first article on stuttering was based on basic general semantic ideas. You can find it at: http://www.masteringstuttering.com/articles/how-to-create-a-good-dose-of-stuttering/.

Foreword

by John C. Harrison

One evening a while ago I received an email from my friend Professor Judith Kuster, who is webmaster for the Stuttering Home Page at Mankato State University.

"I have a challenging little puzzle for you," she wrote. "See if you can solve it. Here are ten numbers. Can you tell me why they're in the order they're in? The numbers are 8549176320."

There was no way I could pass up this challenge. I dropped everything and started wrestling with the puzzle. Now, I pride myself on having a mind that can grasp numbers, even if I can never get my checkbook to balance. I tried everything to make it work. I looked for hidden numerical sequences. I tried dividing numbers by other numbers. I tried multiplying them. I looked for exotic progressions. I wrestled with this conundrum on and off for the better part of two days. No luck. I just couldn't get those numbers to unlock their secret.

Finally, in utter frustration, I wrote back to Judy. "I give up," said. "I need to get a good night's sleep. Tell me the answer."

A little later came her reply, "They're in alphabetical order."

It was so simple. Why couldn't I think of that?

I couldn't think of it because I was stuck in a traditional way of approaching number puzzles. I had made certain unconscious assumptions about how the problem needed to be addressed. I did not know that I had limited my solutions. But the model within which I was working automatically ruled out non-numerical solutions.

This same habit of thinking "inside the box" explains why for the 80 years since the birth of speech pathology, most people have not been able to solve the mystery of stuttering. Our paradigm, or model, of stuttering has forced us to look at the problem through a set of filters that have masked out relevant information and issues. In short, for 80 years, stuttering has been incorrectly characterized, and as a result, most of us have been trying to solve the wrong problem.

I was lucky in that I never went through traditional speech therapy. So my vision was not colored by other people's ideas of what stuttering was all about. Consequently, I ended up foraging on my own for answers, and by the age of 30, I had a different picture of stuttering than virtually anybody else I knew. I had also fully recovered, and this recovery has held for more than 35 years.

What I discovered during my recovery process was that my stuttering was not a speech problem per se, but a problem with *my experience of communicating to others*. That was why I never stuttered when I was alone. I was not communicating with anyone. I also learned that my stuttering not only involved my speech, but all of me, and that included my emotions, perceptions, beliefs, intentions, and physiological responses. These elements were joined together in a spider-like web of interconnections, where a change at any point caused a change at all the other points. In short, I had to look at stuttering as an interactive, dynamic, self-sustaining system. If I wanted to achieve a lasting recovery, I had to address, not just my speech, but the entire system.

Forces that shaped my thinking

An important part of this system was the way I thought about stuttering and about myself. Early in the recovery process, I began to question my way of seeing things. Was the world really such a threatening place, at least on a social level? Or was I creating it that way? Why didn't everyone tense in the presence of authorities? Why didn't other people panic when they had to give their name, or when they had to speak on the telephone to strangers? How was I managing to frame the world in such a negative way?

I eventually discovered that when I blocked, I did so to prevent myself from experiencing things I didn't want to experience. But if it was I who created my speech blocks, then I needed to understand *why* I held myself back and blocked. What was I afraid of? What didn't I want to see? What might happen if I let go? And how could I make my world less threatening?

There were two books back in the early 60s that provided me with a novel way to approach these issues. Both had to do with the running of my mind.

The first was a book called *Psycho-Cybernetics* by a plastic surgeon named Maxwell Maltz. Maltz makes a compelling case for the fact that your unconscious mind accomplishes whatever your conscious mind puts before it – similar to the way a technician programs a computer.

He points out that when confronting a performance fear – such as whether you can make the two-foot putt that wins the golf tournament – if you mentally image only what you're afraid might happen, you'll probably miss the putt. You need to focus all your attention on the desired positive outcome.

The problem is, my mind is also programmed to keep me safe by focusing on any imminent danger, such as the black widow spider on the ceiling or the footsteps behind me as I walk alone at night down a dark street. Not to think about the danger is counter-intuitive. Yet, I must do just that when dealing with a *performance* fear such as stuttering. The book offered some simple but compelling rules for how my mind worked.

The second book, S. I. Hayakawa's *Language in Thought and Action*, was a simplified presentation of general semantics, developed in the 30s by Alfred Korzybski, one of the brilliant minds of the day. General semantics looks at how our habits of thinking color our experiences, and how the structure of language itself forces us to see things in a particular way. Thanks to general semantics, I had a platform from which I could step outside my normal frames of reference and observe and reframe my day-to-day experiences, thus making my world more manageable and less stressful.

Now fast forward 35 years. In early 2002 I received an email from Linda Rounds, a 38-year-old human resources director of a company in Indiana whom I had met over the Internet. Linda wrote to tell me that thanks to my book plus several telephone sessions with a remarkable individual named Bobby Bodenhamer, she had abruptly put an end to a lifelong stuttering problem.

I quickly got in touch with Bob to find out more. It appeared that Bob was a practitioner and teacher of something called neuro-semantics (NS). I discovered that NS is a further development of neuro-linguistic programming (NLP) which, in turn, is a further development of general semantics, the discipline I had found so helpful back in the 60s. Now my interest was really piqued.

It was apparent from the first emails and later, through several phone conversations that Bob Bodenhamer and I were on the same wavelength. Although he had never stuttered himself, Bob had an intuitive understanding of issues that are central to stuttering. This is in part because neuro-semantics, which Bob teaches, addresses the very challenges that I had wrestled with when I was trying to overcome my own stuttering.

I was especially interested in what Bob had to say because, as a person who recovered from stuttering, I have frequently been asked how I got over it. After I tell my story, people naturally ask what they can do to follow in the same path.

Until very recently, I didn't have much to offer when it came to the mind management aspect of stuttering. Maltz's book is still relevant in a general way, but many people want guidance on specific steps they can take to address their blocking. And general semantics, though still valid in its precepts, also does not directly offer specific approaches and exercises on how to address the issues associated with stuttering.

All that has changed with the publication of this book.

A new resource

I Have a Voice is a compendium of concepts and tools that use the principles of Neuro-Semantics to reframe the mindset that leads to speech blocks. Several groups of people will directly benefit from this book.

Therapists and speech-language pathologists who work with those who stutter will find the various neuro-semantic processes and tools extremely helpful. As a practitioner, you'll not only have resources for addressing the physical behaviors of your clients that are counter-productive to fluent speech, but for the first time, you'll have tools for addressing the habits of thought that shape their negative mind state. This is a major resource that has been lacking in the therapist's toolkit. Processes such as those for redefining self, altering states, reframing the meaning of stuttering, and remodeling behavior will now allow you to follow a multi-dimensional approach.

If you're someone who stutters and are motivated to experiment with and explore your own stuttering, you'll also find this book a great resource. You'll acquire workable tools for modifying your mind and emotional states. This, in turn, will help you to counter the feelings of helplessness which are so disempowering and which can make speaking such a troubling experience.

Enterprising individuals who wish to run their own self-therapy program using neuro-semantics resources can be reassured they do not have to go it alone. Thanks to Linda Rounds, who serves as moderator, there is an Internet discussion group on Yahoo where you can share your personal experiences using the principles and precepts described in this book. If you want to participate, you can register at http://groups.yahoo.com/group/neurosemanticsofstuttering. You will also have an opportunity to participate in some of the most intelligent discussions of stuttering-related issues found anywhere on the Internet.

A clarification of terms

Finally, a few observations about the word "stuttering." Although stuttering is a commonly used word, it unfortunately contributes to the confusion because "stuttering" means too many different things.

People who have advanced cases of Parkinsons and who talk in a halting or jerky manner are often referred to as stuttering.

Young children who find themselves linguistically over their head might be labeled as stuttering, even though their speech may be effortless and without any attendant struggle behavior.

Anyone who finds himself upset, confused, uncertain, embarrassed or discombobulated may also have stretches of dysfluency, even though it is totally unself-conscious. I call this *bobulating* to distinguish this form of dysfluency from that in which the individual is momentarily blocked and unable to say a word.

Then there is *blocking*. Without a speech block, there will be no helplessness, frustration, embarrassment, and feelings of disempowerment. The speech block sits at the center of the problem and should not be confused with other kinds of dysfluency.

For reasons of clarity, we encourage people to use the word "blocking" when talking about their speech difficulties. But many remain wedded to the word "stuttering" and are not apt to easily give it up. This is understandable. It's a familiar and commonly used word, and old habits die hard. Consequently, throughout this book, you will see references to the compound word "blocking/stuttering" to distinguish this kind of dysfluency from more general and non-disabling garden varieties of stuttering.

Go at your own pace

A word about the book as a whole. You are not encouraged consume it in one or two sittings. There is too much to think about and too many different processes to absorb in a short time. Rather, it is a reference book rich in understanding and chock full of tools and techniques that can help you get to the heart of you or your client's blocking behaviors and issues. So sip it a bit at a time, live with the information, try out the processes with your clients or with yourself, and if you're someone who stutters, share your thoughts and experiences on the Yahoo group with others of like mind.

Remember that blocking/stuttering is a complex system, and while a person's speech habits substantially contribute to their blocking, their world their view and their habits of thought and perception are likely to be major contributors to the stuttering system and also need to be addressed.

Finally, be prepared for a series of "ah-hah" experiences as you explore blocking/stuttering in a new light and make powerful discoveries about the nature of stuttering and what it takes to recover.

BIOGRAPHY

John C. Harrison showed a marked dysfluency at the age of three and two years later underwent limited therapy. But these efforts were unsuccessful and he ultimately struggled with stuttering throughout college and well into adulthood. Then, in his 20s he immersed himself in a broad variety of personal growth programs, which gave him a unique insight into the nature and dynamics of the stuttering person. As a result, he has been fully recovered for the last 35 years and no longer deals with a stuttering problem.

One of the earliest members of the National Stuttering Association, Harrison was an 18-year member of the Board of Directors and spent nine years as the editor of *Letting GO,* the NSA's monthly newsletter. He has run workshops for the stuttering and the professional communities across the US and Canada as well as in Ireland, the UK, and Australia. He has been published in *Advance Magazine* and the *Journal of Fluency Disorders* and has presented at conventions of the American Speech Language Hearing Association and the California Speech Language Hearing Association, as well as at the First World Congress on Fluency Disorders in Munich, Germany.

Harrison lives with his wife in San Francisco where he works as a presentation coach, speaker, and freelance writer. He also coaches people by phone on how to investigate, understand and transform the system that creates and maintains their stuttering system.

Introduction

I did not plan to work with people who block and stutter. Indeed, it happened quite by accident. Some years ago, a sales seminar participant asked me if I could help people who stutter. I told him that I didn't know, but I sure would be glad to give it a try. His son, Charles, then twenty-five, came in for a two hour session. After one hour's work we discovered that behind his blocking and stuttering were some fears of speaking that were rooted in childhood. Once he realized that he was mentally causing the stutter, he thanked me, paid me and left. And as far as I know, he gained complete fluency. The key for him was understanding that *he* was creating the stuttering, that it was neither something physical nor out of his control.

I have been working as a practitioner of Neuro-Linguistic Programming (NLP) since 1990. A major component of my work has been in dealing with fears, anxiety and phobias. Over those 14 years I have worked with hundreds of clients – approximately three thousand hours of therapy. NLP offers a model for understanding and for changing the way someone makes meaning of their experience, based on how they perceive their world in terms of language, thoughts, states and behaviors. NLP offers effective techniques which can be used widely: in therapy, sales, management, relationships, and, yes, for dealing with stuttering and much more. You will learn more about how change happens as the book unfolds.

Excited about the results with Charles, I wrote up a case study of the therapy and sent it to my colleague Michael Hall. He expanded this case study into an article, "Meta-Stating Stuttering: Approaching Stuttering Using NLP and Neuro-Semantics", which I then posted on our website:
http://www.neurosemantics.com/Articles/Stuttering.htm

After posting the article, I was contacted by a friend of mine whom I had worked with early in my practice. We had worked on his stuttering years earlier but that hadn't helped him. After reading the article he called me and asked me if I had learned something new. I told him that I sure had and for him to come on over.

Six months after our one hour session I saw him again and asked him how the stuttering was. He paused briefly, wrinkled his brow, and replied, "I guess I have forgotten to stutter." "Well," I said, "that sure is a great thing to forget to do."

Needless to say, I was elated with that outcome. However, the major breakthrough came in the spring of 2002 when Linda Rounds emailed me from Indiana. In her search to overcome her stuttering she had read a work by Anthony Robbins at the recommendation of John Harrison. From Anthony Robbins she learned about NLP, so she searched Amazon.com for NLP books and found the book I co-authored with Michael Hall, *The User's Manual for the Brain*. From that she obtained my email address and wrote to ask me if I could assist her. In just a few therapy sessions on the phone and via some emails, Linda gained complete fluency. Wow, was I excited. As a result, Linda and I wrote an article entitled "From Stuttering to Stability: A Case Study." John Harrison published the article in the National Stuttering Association newsletter, *Letting Go*. I have included the complete article in Appendix B.

Because of this article I have had the opportunity to work with several People Who Stutter (PWS), including the speech pathologist Tim Mackesey, SLP (Speech Language Pathologist). It was somewhat ironic to assist to fluency a speech pathologist who had blocked and stuttered most of his life. Tim is now using my techniques in his own practice near Atlanta, Georgia, working with people who block and stutter.

Tim's website is: www.stuttering-specialist.com.

Let me say up front that not everyone has attained fluency but many have. Importantly, out of all the people I have worked with, I am confident that all of them have the capacity to attain fluency eventually, just so long as they continue working on their *thinking*.

Chapter One

The Origins of Stuttering

How blocking begins

In every case I have worked with, the roots of the individual's blocking are in childhood. Sometimes however, the actual blocking does not appear until adolescence or even adulthood. People who block usually refer to their non-fluency as *blocking* or *stuttering* (*stammering* in the UK). In itself, this is no problem. It is when they come to believe that blocking is something bad and to be feared that problems arise.

CASE STUDY 1

Susan was very angry with her parents because she believed that if they had not gotten all upset about her childhood problem of learning how to speak, then she would not have started blocking and stuttering. I encouraged Susan to speak with her mother about it. Here is Susan's reply:

Well I did it! I spoke to my mom about my stuttering and it was not bad. I actually feel some peace. It is not complete, but better. I was afraid to talk to her but I did. We talked about stuttering openly but we didn't talk about the touchy-feely stuff. I said I'd been very angry and explained how the work I do sometimes increases my feeling of anger because I think she could have behaved better. I was able to show empathy and to see it through her eyes. I think my parents did try a lot of things and I don't think it was in the vengeful way that I always see. I think the way I chose to see things is definitely holding me back.

My mother was OK with this talk and actually supportive. I told her that I feel she still has feelings of embarrassment about my stuttering and she said, "I don't worry about you, in my eyes you have made it, you are successful living a life and that's all we wanted for you." That was a shock to hear. Maybe I don't get that I have already arrived in some ways in the work that I have done. I think I have refused to see that. I also realized that I don't want to spend the rest of my life talking about my stuttering – there is more to life. I think I am too attached to my stuttering.

Sometimes I think it is a way to shield myself from my true feelings and relations to people. You are so busy thinking and being obsessed with stuttering that you don't need to think about your feelings, it is a good feeling blocker. John Harrison said it is so much about feelings and not about stuttering. I never understood that before.

Susan's story is typical of People Who Stutter (PWS). Her story illustrates the theme of this book: that stuttering is a learned behavior, and, as such, can be unlearned. However, much speech therapy in the United States addresses the symptoms rather than the cause, the physical components of blocking and stuttering and not the underlying meanings that the person has given to blocking and stuttering.

Childhood experiences

In that the origins of blocking and stuttering arise from emotional hurts experienced during childhood, the PWS is no different from the other people who seek my assistance. They all demonstrate a similar structure of learned negative associations which they are unable to control consciously. Although it is possible that a child has some kind of disfluency as a result of genetic defects, it is more likely that their disfluency is just the normal stumbling with words as the child learns how to speak. However, should a parent or significant other adult think that the child has a speech problem, the child is told that they stutter and off to the speech pathologist they go. This confirms to the child that there is something unacceptable about their speech, and something wrong or unacceptable about *them*.

I have yet to find a person who fell in love with their stuttering. If every time they experience difficulty speaking they think of this as something bad, then over time this badness becomes a habit, and they generalize that badness to themselves. One question you could ask is "How do you know this is bad? Who told you?" The knowledge that their speech is abnormal usually comes from a parent or significant other person pointing out that there is something wrong with how they speak. (However, I have found a few people who block and stutter who placed the "bad" and "unacceptable" label on themselves without any knowledge of outside influences.)

Susan is a good example of this. She thinks that being dragged to a speech pathologist solidified her perception that she was flawed in some way, and that she had to be "perfect" in speech in order for her mother and father to like her.

Children who block describe non-fluency as something they wish to avoid or control. They may have reached their own conclusion on this, or based it on what adults or their peers have said. In addition, their blocking is connected to the negative emotions which accompanied some earlier painful experiences associated with not being fluent in speech. Many times the PWS will describe their experiences as being traumatic. Having friends mock you, or school teachers embarrassed because of how you speak can also "lock in the block." Indeed, when a teacher stands a child up before a class and shouts "Spit it out!", for the child who is trying to talk but can't, it is trauma.

The precipitating event may not be something terrible or tragic; the child may have interpreted the divorce of the parents, the lack of affection from dad, the lack of emotional support from mom, or any emotional and physical abuse as being painful and threatening. The child does what all children tend to do – they personalize the external problems, assume some degree of responsibility, and then internalize and express the hurt in the muscles used for breathing/speaking. They begin to block.

Blocking is also connected with feelings of helplessness in not being able to speak when required to. This leads to feeling that you are different or strange – something children wish to avoid at all cost. From these childhood experiences the child learns that blocking and stuttering is unacceptable behavior, and grows up fearing that they will continue to block. The fear itself creates even more blocking and stuttering. Essentially, the PWS "becomes that which they fear most."

This book is includes ways of identifying those painful emotions and suggests means of healing them.

The concept of self

A person's concept of self grows and changes throughout their life-time. It is first formalized by their caregivers who named them and began to relate to them as a separate individual. The child needs a firm foundation of how the world works. During their early years they do not critically filter incoming information because they have yet to develop the ability to *think about, reflect on* or *question* their experience. Instead, what they learn in childhood becomes their truth – and that proves both a blessing and a curse. Sometimes the child gets hold of the wrong end of the stick, as it were, when making meaning of their own behaviors, and that meaning may endure. The blocking then persists because the PWS continues to think in a "childish" way: the meaning of their behavior still relates to those early years experiences.

The same is true for practically all emotional problems that adults have. The issues I deal with therapeutically come from thinking patterns the clients learned in childhood. Allowing other people to determine your concept of self is appropriate when you are a young child, but not desirable as you mature. One solution to this problem is to get the PWS to grow up those parts of themselves which are stuck in childhood. The person first needs to practice mentally stepping back so that they may critically examine the beliefs they have carried with them since childhood. They use their adult mind to notice how they have constructed their model of the world, the beliefs that enable them to function, and then to update any which are obsolete.

One of the most debilitating beliefs of a PWS is their claim to know how other people perceive them. Yet they never check the truth or accuracy of such claims. I have discovered with people who block that the typical self-definition they received from others is based on mind-reading: they believe that other people view them as weird, dumb, different, mentally retarded, and so on. They take this on board, assume this information is accurate, and then live as if those self-descriptions are true. *In their fear of being judged by others, they are in fact themselves unfairly judging others.*

The Body-Mind connection

This connection is obvious in the most primitive of all mind-body functions, the fight/flight arousal pattern. You don't have to be in actual danger to set it off. Simply remember or imagine something fearful and your body will respond by producing adrenalin. We find linguistic evidence of the connection in the expressions: gut feeling, pain in the neck, heartfelt, get things off your chest, and so on.

Those early negative influences concerning the child's speech become grooved into the child's muscles and are carried into adulthood. By "grooved into the muscles" I refer to someone's ability to learn unconsciously; it is as though what we learn literally becomes embodied into our muscle tissue (referred to as *muscle memory*). For example, if you touch-type, and I ask you where the R key is, how will you locate it? Did your left index finger twitch and move up to the left? That would be an example of "in the muscle" learning.

Because people who stutter tend to feel the fears or anxieties that contribute to their blocking in the muscles that control breathing and speaking, I propose that blocking is similar in structure to panic and anxiety attacks. This means that the treatment could also be similar because emotions have become expressed in the body.

Over the years of doing therapy, I have asked hundreds of clients, "Where in your body do you feel that negative emotion?" Usually the PWS who feels a negative emotion can pinpoint the area of the body where they feel that emotion. There have been very few instances when the person was unable to tell me exactly where they felt it. Check this for yourself. Think of something you fear or recall a recent emotional hurt. Then notice where in your body that emotion finds expression.

For people who block, negative emotions are typically centered within the chest, neck and/or jaw. Ask a person who blocks:

- Which emotions have you associated with your blocking?
- Where in your body do you feel these emotions?
- Where in you body do you feel the fear and anxiety as you anticipate the possibility of blocking?
- What do you think *about* these feelings?

As these feelings diminish, the blocking and stuttering also lessen and the person becomes more fluent.

Not every client accepts that their emotions are created – a product of thought – rather than real. "But, Dr Bob, I 'feel' that anxiety in my body and if I feel it, it must be real!" That is the normal response: if I feel it, it is real. For the PWS, the emotions around blocking and stuttering are more real than that for they have the strong physiological response associated with blocking and stuttering. So no wonder many in the speech pathology profession believe that stuttering is a physical problem. It is so *real*: "Just look at my facial contortions when I block."

CASE STUDY 2

John Harrison, a person who stuttered and who recovered, is the former editor of the National Stuttering Association's newsletter, *Letting GO*. In his article, "Anatomy of a Block" (Harrison, 1999) he exquisitely illustrates how a person feels a total loss of power and resourcefulness especially during blocking. John has graciously given me permission to share his article with you. The first part of his article reproduced here:

One day back in the spring of 1982 I walked into a camera shop on 24th street near where I live in San Francisco to pick up some prints. The clerk, a pretty young girl, was at the other end of the counter, and when I came in, she strolled over to wait on me.

"What's your name?" she asked.

That question used to throw me into a panic, because I always blocked on my name. Always. But by 1982 stuttering was no longer an issue. I never thought about it. I liked talking to people, and never worried about speech, because my blocks had all but disappeared.

I started to say "Harrison", and suddenly found myself in a panic. I was locked up and totally blocked. All the old, familiar feelings had come back. I could feel my heart pounding. So I stopped, took a breath, allowed myself to settle down, and, while the woman stared at me, collected myself enough to say "Harrison."

I walked out of the store with my prints, feeling frazzled and totally mystified. Where in the world had that block come from? Why had I suddenly fallen into the old pattern? Stuttering was the furthest thing from my mind when I walked in. I never thought about stuttering any more, because it never happened, so I knew it wasn't a fear of stuttering that caused me to block. At that point I did what I had always done in previous years when stuttering was a problem. I began playing the event over and over in my mind, trying to notice as much detail as possible to see if I could spot any clues, something that would explain what was going on.

"Where was the woman when I walked in?" I asked myself.

Let's see. I pictured the layout of the store. I had come in and stood at the cash register. The woman was at the other end of the counter talking to someone.

"Who was the other person? Anything significant in that?"

It was a guy.

"And what did he look like?" Hmmm. Oh yeah, he was a biker. Tough looking. Had tattoos on his arms and was wearing a Levi's vest.

"What else did you notice?"

Well, the two of them seemed to like talking to each other. The guy appeared very much taken with the girl.

"How did he seem to you?"

Scary looking. Reminded me of the tough guys on the block when I was a kid. I remember those guys. They lived in the next town. They all had mean looking eyes, and they petrified me.

"How did you respond to people like him when you were a kid?"

Well, if I were on the street when several tough guys passed by, I would make myself invisible so they couldn't see me and hassle me. I'd suck all my energy in. I'd blend into the background. I'd look like a tree, or a bush, or a brick wall. No energy would radiate from me until they had passed. Nothing.

"Did you have any other feelings or observations about the biker in the store?"

I guess I felt like I'd interrupted an important conversation, because the two of them were getting on so well together.

"How did that make you feel?"

I reviewed the scene once more, trying to recall how I felt. How did I feel? I really concentrated, and a malaise swept across me. Then it came to me. I was worried that he'd be irked because the girl had left him to wait on me.

"So what was your response in such situations when you were a kid?"

I'd hold back. I didn't want to stand out. I didn't want to seem too strong or too assertive.

"Because ...."

Because it would put me in danger. The guy might give me trouble, so I didn't want him to "see" me.

"So in the camera store you ...."

Right. I slipped back into the old program. I held back. I blocked my energy. I tried to make myself invisible, just like in the old days.

Here John clearly explains from a personal standpoint how something can trigger an old memory that mentally and emotionally sent him back to his childhood. Ceasing being an adult with adult resources, John says, "The memories triggered a fight or flight reaction that I managed by holding back (blocking) my feelings and pushing the thoughts out of awareness."

No longer responding as an adult, John responded out of those old childhood memories of powerlessness. When in the presence of that tough looking biker, John unconsciously flew back in time and regressed into the kid who was petrified by the "tough guys on the block." So John the grown man became as *powerless* as a little kid confronted by bullies.

Because people operate from their perception of reality, which is based on their unique way of making meaning of the world, then the strategies they have for intervening in the world in order to change it will depend upon what they think is possible.

Emotions

Evaluating your experience often produces some kind of emotional response. For example, you may become angry that you are stuck, and that you are unable to do anything. Being angry does not help; it is what you are now feeling, and your emotions tend to permeate your whole being. Emotions are related to your *judgments* and *values*. When you evaluate your experience as good, you experience positive emotions. If, on the other hand, your experience of the world does not validate your expectations, values, dreams and desires, you tend to experience negative emotions such as frustration, anger, and resentment.

In their early years children *expect* love and acceptance from the significant people around them, but often find that they are rejected for whatever reason. Actually, being rejected is inevitable; it is part of growing up. You cannot depend on others forever; at some point you have to make your own way in the world. It therefore matters how you learn to deal with rejection. Fluent communication requires a great deal of practice. There are many times in the early years when children are learning to speak when they stumble and stutter as they express themselves. If the PWS learns to associate rejection from others with a particular behaviour –

their blocking and stuttering – then the emotions surrounding that become dominant, and the child pays more and more attention to the way they are speaking. What would happen to their speech if the PWS refused to generate these negative emotions? Well, they could get on and practice their speaking skills, knowing that they will learn from their failures – as they would in other areas of their lives. That's what growing up is about.

Because you create your emotions based on an evaluation of your experience of the world at any given moment, your emotions are only accurate for that moment. You had an experience; you either got what you expected and felt good about it, or your expectations were frustrated and you felt bad about it. However, when the emotions from one experience color other experiences you may be generalizing inappropriately. For instance, if as a child their peers teased them for blocking and stuttering, the PWS may have then evaluated that as a hurtful and judged their peers as spiteful. This leads to poor relationships and ineffective communication in the future. When the PWS is teased in adulthood – because that's what some adults do – it reminds them of their earlier experiences of being made fun of, and triggers the same emotional response. In this way, they amalgamate all the meanings and judgments associated with their present and their past, and they make unchecked assumptions about the other person's intentions. They engage in a form of *mind-reading*: assuming they know what another person is thinking. The PWS frequently mind-reads other people as judging them because they stutter. In other words, the PWS relies on their own fantasies, pays attention only to their own thoughts, rather than putting their attention on the outside world and checking out their ideas with those other people.

Unconscious competence

You probably know how to drive a car, play tennis, ride a bicycle, send an email. Every skills becomes, so to speak, grooved into your muscles through repetition. You have neural pathways for changing gear, for serving at tennis, for using a keyboard. Each skill engages a different set of muscles. It is also the case that your level of skill in each activity will depend to some extent on your mental state, your level of commitment or concentration, the degree to which you are thinking about what you are doing and so on. With practice, many such skills become automatic, and you do them without thinking. Indeed, when you are faced with returning a high velocity tennis ball you don't have time to think. You trust your muscles have been sufficiently grooved through practice so that you can continue the volley.

The PWS has not only learned how to block, they have also learned how to be fluent, and both activities they perform automatically. As with playing tennis, they have separate neural pathways for engaging with others and for managing their state. They respond differently according to the situation. While alone or speaking to someone with whom they are comfortable, the neural pathway for fluency is activated. However, when the context triggers fear and anxiety, the neural pathway for blocking is triggered. In both cases they have options; both neural pathways are there, but only one is active.

Your state of mind affects your behavior. During the day you experience many states, both highs and lows, pro-active and re-active. When blocking, the PWS's state of mind tends towards re-active fear and anxiety. But in fluency they have pro-active states of mind built on calmness, trust, and curiosity, and they focus more on *what* they are communicating to others rather than *how* they are performing. Fluency states are more likely to produce enjoyment and the feeling of empowerment. Therefore the aim is to lead the PWS to change their responses so that they automatically and habitually activate the fluency response in all situations. One way of doing this is through *reframing* – transforming the meaning of the situation (see Chapter Six) – so that the PWS comes to minimize those frames of meaning that have "locked in the block". However, this requires repeated practice. There is no magic cure. For fluency to become the PWS's natural way of being, they will have to make many changes in both body and mind.

Freezing

Like all muscles, [the diaphragm] tends to contract as a response to fear. Unfortunately, the diaphragm needs to relax in order to speak. You have two powerful forces trying to move the diaphragm in opposite directions. You have the natural response to fear contracting the diaphragm and drawing air in. Then you have your own desire to speak trying to relax the diaphragm so that air can move over the vocal cords. The result is what? A frozen diaphragm, of course.

McGuire 2002: 21

Emotions such as fear profoundly affect the entire body-mind system. The fight or flight mechanism pumps adrenalin into the body for increased muscle power so that the person can run away or defend their ground. However, another response is that the person freezes to the spot. They describe themselves as being like a deer looking into the headlights. Even though the fight or flight response has been activated, all action is inhibited: they believe they have no options for action open to them. Their speaking also freezes.

Because they are no longer doing anything, this freeze-state can become associated with how they are thinking *about* their condition, with the judgments they are making about their own (lack of) performance and with the doom-laden consequences of being frozen or blocked in this way: "I can't get out of this! I'm going to be blocking for the rest of my life!" That reinforces their self-evaluation that: "There is something wrong with me." Instead of paying attention to the outside world, they are focusing on their inner thoughts, feelings, and imaginings. They are relating to themselves rather than to the other person, and shutting out potentially useful information from the world around them.

There is an alternative. Being frozen gives them time to choose some resourceful states and apply those to themselves (which I call *meta-stating*). There is a general sense that "the good guys win" when it comes to states. By immersing yourself in a positive, supportive and resourceful state, it will dominate the *fear* and *anxiety* and suppress or even eliminate them. What happens when you apply *faith* or *courage* to fear? (See Chapter Three.) One of the key factors in learning how to run your own mind is in managing your own states. You are teaching your body to activate life enhancing states more often so that your response to any internal or external trigger will be desirable.

Childhood needs

Blocking served some vital childhood need. It is highly probable that that need is no longer relevant, but you still need to check. If the need is still current, then find out from the PWS what it does for them, so that they can find alternative ways of meeting it. Susan (Case Study 1) went on to say:

Today, when doing my journaling about life, something came up about stuttering. In fact, I even drew some pictures to express my feelings. I was journaling about how my stuttering is keeping me from where I want to go with my business. I actually drew a cage and put myself in it. When I am in the cage I think the following:

- Oh, I stutter, I can't do that.
- Oh that is too big for me. Oh, wait a minute, I have to be fluent for that.
- Oh, I can't function in the business world; they will laugh at my stuttering.
- I can't handle success, it is too much.

Then I also drew several blue circles around my body, like a mummy would be taped up. I called it my *stutter suit*. I put this on when I am scared. When I have my stutter suit on I think the following thoughts:

- *I am protected.*
- *No one can hurt me.*
- *I am protected* from all those possibilities of the unknown."
- *I can control my blocking.*
  [Italics added. See also Alan's story in Case Study 7]

Why would anybody want to stutter? How in the world can anybody get any kind of gain out of stuttering? And yet when you ask people how they benefit – "What do you get out of blocking?" – they give meaningful answers. In other words, blocking has to provide some benefit or else the person wouldn't do it! It is therapeutically useful to assume that every behavior has a positive intention, that people do things because in *their* model of the world there is some positive or beneficial outcome for them. For example, if you elicit the positive intention for blocking, you discover that at a younger age it provided protection, attention, a sense of control, or revenge – which are probably no longer appropriate in their adult life.

With problematic behaviors like blocking and stuttering, the present behavior provides little that is positive for the person. You often have to look back to the origins of the behavior to find its positive intent at that time. At its inception the stuttering provided a solution to the problem the person was experiencing then. It changed the meaning of the situation and reduced the negative emotions being generated. The four positive intentions which I have encountered most frequently are that blocking and stuttering:

- Protect me from being hurt.
- Get me attention, make people notice me.
- Provide the PWS a sense of having some control: "I cannot control this sick family but I can control my speech. I will block."
- Provide a way to "get back" at parents, teachers, therapists or peers.

CASE STUDY 3

Josh grew up in the home where neither parents knew how to give and receive love. Josh's mother would reach out to him pretending to provide him with love and encouragement, but when Josh responded she would push him away. He queried, "How do I please her without being ridiculed, hit, or put in the corner?"

Later Josh spoke to his father about this. His father confirmed that when Josh was a small toddler his mother would indeed ridicule him, hit him, and put him in the corner of the room. This behavior of Josh's mother created intense fear, insecurity and anger in him. All of these emotions became associated with his blocking and stuttering. I asked Josh to re-experience that intense fear, insecurity and anger. I then inquired of Josh the purpose for his stuttering. He immediately responded, "Stuttering is a way for me to strike back at the bitch. I want to make it frustrating and uncomfortable for her."

14

This concept is extremely important. In order to bring about change, we must first find out the purpose of the behavior the person is wanting to change. If their behavior is producing a valid response to their need it is unlikely that they will change that behavior unless and until that need is being met in another, healthier way. For instance, in Josh's case, he first needs to *let go* of the need to avenge his mother. Forgiveness is more likely when the person is able to dissociate from this involvement. Having a degree of objectivity about a key relationship enables them to find the necessary resources and reframe the meaning of that experience. These techniques are covered later in this book.

Josh's need for vengeance fulfils a childhood purpose. He has to release this if he is to become more adult in his way of dealing with this relationship. Josh has no need for blocking or stuttering when he is able to forgive his mother and apply adult resources to the need for attention and protection. Essentially, he is growing up that part of him responsible for the childish behavior. The patterns in this book provide ways for healing the hurt behind such memories and for providing new ways for people to get what they want with blocking and stuttering.

Reasons for blocking and stuttering

Children at school not only have their peers making fun of them because they stutter, they may also find school-teachers ridiculing them in front of the class. A history of such experiences can produce layers of hurt that locks in the block. Eventually the children *identify* with blocking and stuttering: "I am different. I really am." "There is something wrong with me." "I am useless." "I am worthless." "I am a weirdo."

Some children deliberately choose to stutter because that is a way of protecting themselves within a dysfunctional family or in a hostile school environment. One client chose to block and stutter as a child in order to make things uncomfortable for his parents because they made life uncomfortable for him. As he grew through childhood and adolescence, the fear and insecurity he had acquired to cope with his sick family preserved his blocking and stuttering. Overcoming the problem was consequently a real challenge.

Another client, whose mother smothered her as a child, started blocking and stuttering because she thought that the behaviour would *control* her very controlling mother. She also discovered that blocking and stuttering served her as an *attention getter* from those people around her.

As a clinician, be aware that the form of the childhood blocking and stuttering will vary for each person. So treat each client as a unique individual, rather than simply generalizing across all clients. It is only when you understand the structure of how each one blocks and stutters that you can design your interventions for their particular need.

CASE STUDY 4

Although the vast majority of people start blocking and stuttering in childhood, there are the rare PWS who begin when they are adult. For example, I received the following email from Matt:

I have a great deal of experience in Public Speaking … and, until recently, typically presented at over 100–150 Investor Seminars per year. About 4–6 months ago, I developed a stuttering "habit", which seems to rear its head primarily while talking on the telephone … although a few times in front of a crowd.

It's not a severe problem, but I find it somewhat annoying … I have actually begun to initiate "avoidance behavior" when it comes to speaking on the phone with people I don't know too well. Two months ago I decided to make a career change (within the same firm) to become an Investment Advisor. (The career change was unrelated to the stuttering.)

I'm somewhat apprehensive and concerned about the obvious necessity of dealing with clients on the telephone … as this is naturally, a huge part of running an advisory business practice … and prospecting.

Matt's first experience with stuttering began in adulthood. I have not spoken to him in detail but I did ask him in a second email to check out what it was he was so fearful about when speaking on the phone:

> This statement is very provocative to me ... since I don't feel that I'm fearful of anything *more than the possibility of stuttering* ... and the stuttering began at a time when I was questioning my passion for my career ... and was particularly stressed with 18–20 hour work days. [italics added]

In the third email I inquired:

> If you didn't have the fear of the 'possibility of stuttering' what would change?

He replied:

> I would be able to fluently and easily pick up the phone and speak with anyone and everyone without having the nervousness and apprehension which comes with the fear that I may not be able to communicate properly and get stuck over words. I would actually enjoy the experience of getting to know new people and conveying the Investment principles that I truly believe in.

Not being able to cope with dealing with clients on the phone suggests it is highly likely that the roots are in his childhood. Such behavior frequently indicates lack of confidence and that usually arises from a poor self-image. However, that can be changed. For example, Susan completed her story as follows:

> Then I drew another picture. I was still in cage but stutter suit was off. The following thoughts were present:
>
> * I can make phone calls.
> * I can look people straight in the eyes.
> * I can stay in the moment of stuttering.
> * I can love myself for who I am, if I stutter or not.

> Then I went a step further with the stutter suit off. I stepped out of the box and immediately I was in an empowered state. Here were my thoughts:
>
> • I am empowered, I am out of jail.
> • I can be real and all that I am. I can anything, there are no limits.
> • I can really rock.
> • There is so much I can do.
>
> It is so amazing, how these 2 different states really create different results. It is really neat!

Three keys to fluency

In working with PWS I have come to the conclusion that there are three key steps towards more fluency. The PWS must:

1. Develop a healthy concept of Self, especially within the context of stuttering.
2. Ignore what others may or may not think about them. Not be bothered by how other people talk about them.
3. Know that they have the personal resources necessary for living successfully in the world.

Of these, the first step is fundamental. It is only when the PWS has developed an inner sense of worth and self-esteem that they can ignore what others may or may not think or say about how they speak. When that fear goes, most if not all of blocking and stuttering goes with it.

The PWS crucially begins to overcome that ingrained habit by building a healthy view of themselves. In this book there are several exercises designed to assist you to lead a PWS towards a healthier view of themselves so that they can be fluent in all contexts.

Using what you already have

I have a simple theory: "If a person can speak fluently in one context, then that person can learn to speak fluently in all contexts." People who stutter already know how to talk; they do not need to re-learn how to do this. What they need is to be able to access the same state of mind they are in when they are speaking fluently.

Blocking does not happen all the time. It is only triggered in those contexts where the PWS has associated fear and/or anxiety. The emotional issues which contribute to blocking and stuttering are reinforced through experiences such as bullying, teasing, being ridiculed, and so on. Most if not all PWS fear what others will think of them if they block and stutter. They tend to define their concept of self based on this behavior and believe: "I am different, so there is something wrong with me." Many PWS feel powerless to overcome this problem. They tend to believe that the world in which they live is filled with people who are out to get them.

Throughout life, bonds of various strengths are created between your experiences and your emotions, and these find expression in your body. Those which are repeated, both negative and positive, become stronger. It seems highly probable that the feelings which are connected to blocking affect the breathing and speaking muscles. In that way, blocking is similar to a panic or anxiety attack. However, a person who has panic attacks does not live every moment of every day panicking. Similarly, the person who blocks and stutters is not always blocking. As with a panic attack, blocking is triggered psychologically. Therefore the way to change this response is to change the cognitive aspects of this learned behavior.

The average PWS has spent years achieving mastery – they can block without thinking about it! To change this habit, they will need to spend time practicing flying into states of calm (see Chapter Five). The vast majority of clients with anxiety problems whom I have seen over the years took up to twelve hours of therapy to eliminate the fear or at least make it manageable. It then required three months or more practicing changing their focus of attention. However, it may take longer with PWS. Not all completely overcome their problem; a few hardly change at all.

Although I highly recommend that you work face-to-face with clients because that provides important visual information, much can still be achieved through telephone consultations. It is surprising how much can be done auditorily, even though this is the area of difficulty! After 25–30 hours and much practice, several PWS have gained either normal fluency or are greatly improved. Why does change take so long? Because these emotions and strategies are so well programmed into the body, and it takes time for the body to readjust to cognitive changes.

Because blocking and stuttering are learned behaviors, they can be unlearned. A practical way of doing this is through the use of cognitive (thinking) techniques such as those of Neuro-Linguistic Programming (NLP) and Neuro-Semantics®, both of which are primarily cognitive therapies. This book includes those processes which I have used successfully with clients who suffered from anxiety and panic disorders. These two methodologies provide ways of working to change blocking and stuttering behaviours by altering the way someone thinks.

By changing the thinking-and-feeling components of experience you can effect change in the messages that the body-mind sends to refresh and reinforce the neural pathways. This offers hope for recovery and transformation. It is therefore not surprising that in the past three decades the many forms of Cognitive Behavioral Therapy (CBT) have been instrumental in creating the most significant changes. The Neuro-Semantics model has enabled us to pioneer faster and more streamlined ways of getting to the source of the problem – the cognitive frames that determine experience.

The aim is to remove the debilitating meaning of particular people and events so that they no longer fear them, but act fluently and confidently. Changing the PWS's cognitive frames necessitates helping them reframe all those unconscious hurts and fears around stuttering (see Chapter Five). It's not that the PWS has to be super-aware of their behavior. On the contrary, they eventually become totally bored with or indifferent to that dysfunctional behavior so that they ignore it, let it go, and do something more interesting. They establish and maintain good relationships with others; they communicate by paying more attention to the other person. This is, after all, what makes life worth living.

Chapter Two

Learning to Think Differently

If blocking is primarily cognitive rather than physiological, then it seems sensible to find ways of resolving this problem through cognitive means. This means that the PWS needs to change the way they think about themselves, how they relate to others, and how they fulfil their needs. Until they change how they think about stuttering, their physiology will stay the same.

A key change comes from acknowledging that you have control over what you think. Once you accept that the cause of the blocking lies in the way you think, this offers you the means to solve your problems. It also stops the foolishness of believing other people control your mind without your permission. When the PWS is able to say *Yes* to the belief: "No one can make me believe or feel anything that I choose not to believe or feel" and incorporate it into their model of the world, the fear of what other people may think of them disappears. Once that belief about other people *causing* them to stutter is out of the way the PWS realizes that they have to take responsibility for creating their own stuttering. Then there is no reason for the stuttering to persist

Although changing your thinking can sometimes happen quickly, it is more often the case that it takes time, especially if the PWS is adjusting their responses to childhood hurts which have been very well learned. Your role is to help them build the necessary skills step by step: undoing old thought patterns and learning new ones so that the old fears and other negative emotions around blocking diminish. For a start, the PWS must stop telling themselves negative stories and instead learn how to access resource states and apply them when needed.

All the change patterns and processes in this book are intended to enable you to assist the PWS to find their own resources which will enable them to function well. One byproduct of working with PWS to access the numerous resources they already have available within themselves, is that they also become more attuned to the present. Once the PWS can give a great big *No* to those old child-hood limiting beliefs and a great big *Yes* to their present adult resources they will be moving rapidly towards increasing fluency. Having changed the meaning of those situations which used to lead to blocking, they learn to interpret their experience in more flexible ways, and have more effective strategies for getting what they want. Indeed, this is true for all therapy.

Meaning

In order to operate in the world you need to make meaning of your experience. A meaningful experience is one that provides an opportunity for taking action. It doesn't mean that you will be successful, only that you have a strategy for intervention. People are happy when they can interpret a situation and know what to do. Because any situation can be interpreted in a number of ways, it matters how people interpret what is happening because the meaning they give it determines what they will actually do.

The word "meaning" comes from an Old High German word meaning "to hold in mind". Because much of what we hold in mind is linguistic, it matters how we use language, how we talk to ourselves, because the meanings are in the form of stories about how to do things and "what happens next". These stories create our model of the world, hold everything in place (at least temporarily), and thus influence the whole body-mind system. The PWS has meanings which hold blocking and stuttering in place. Once those particular meanings are removed or changed, other strategies or stories – resources – become available, and the blocking and stuttering behaviors lose their power and disappear.

Every visual image, sound, feeling, smell, taste and word has associations for us. Every experience leads to a composite of meanings and mind-body states. Over the years we learn to associate particular experiences with certain body-mind states, both pleasurable and inhibitory. For example, a favorite meal may not only stimulate appetite, but also remind you of pleasant memories of previous meals in good company in beautiful surroundings.

Alternatively, people may avoid situations when something unpleasant occurred because that triggers upsetting memories.

However, some common situations cannot be avoided because they are part of everyday life. Personal history is powerful: "I have always blocked and I always will." So when the PWS encounters the kind of person with whom they usually block, a limiting state arises and they actually block. Other triggers could be the way someone looks, such as having a confused look on their face, starting to snigger, or acting as if they are in a hurry. The PWS connects their feeling response to that with particular context: the appearance, voice tonality or behavior of the other person.

To find out what kind of anchors trigger their blocking, just ask the PWS, "How do you know when to block?" "What triggers you to block?" Because blocking is not inevitable, you could assume that when those key factors are missing they are fluent. Check that out: "And when you are fluent, that key factor is not present?" In this way the PWS discovers what sets off their blocking behavior. Then they can choose to change the meaning and power of those triggers. This makes a profound difference to someone's life. Once on the road to fluency, the old meanings associated with blocking simply dissolve.

The following situations commonly trigger blocking for most PWS:

- Being away from the safety of being by themselves at home.
- Finding the atmosphere "tense" or "serious".
- Being under pressure to finish what they have to say. Having to "Hurry up!"
- Reading out loud in front of a group.
- Speaking to anyone at all/anyone in authority/anyone of the opposite sex.
- Ordering in a restaurant, or asking a shop assistant for help.
- Making a phone call or answering the telephone. (Some can make a call but cannot answer the phone, and vice versa. It depends on the meaning of the context.)

What exactly is the trigger? Sometimes it is a combination of factors; the PWS interprets the whole situation together with their expectations as the cue for running their blocking strategy. It may be that they are no longer aware of what the specific cues are because they have generalized the situation. For example, it is sufficient that they perceive the other person as having higher status, an "authority figure", or in a position of power over them. The PWS explains this by saying that it goes back to their childhood, being confronted or challenged by the parents, or perhaps to a time when they were being put down by teachers. Since then it has been extended to all other people in authority. The thought now serves as the trigger for the PWS to experience blocking.

Beliefs about self

The PWS usually has a number of limiting beliefs about who they are, and come to identify with the negative descriptions of themselves which they connect to the blocking and stuttering.

CASE STUDY 5

Sam had stuttered since a small child. He grew up in a nation that was under attack from a neighboring more powerful nation. If this wasn't bad enough, Sam grew up in a home where his parents constantly fought. He had clear memories of being in his bedroom listening to his parents fighting.

The insecurities arising from their hostility had a more profound effect on Sam than did his memories of hearing bombs explode. That says something about the importance of growing up in a secure environment.

Sam developed such beliefs as:

- "There is no meaning to life. The more I achieve, the less I feel fulfilled."
- "Marriage is the end of love because it creates a miserable life."
- "No one can have enough girls." (If marriage is the end of love, how could anyone settle down with only one woman?)
- "The only way one can find fulfillment is to die."
- "People who are happy are kidding themselves."

- "Nothing will make me happy."
- "Life is 'exile'."
- "People who are nice are not real."
- "People who are ugly and mean are real."

Those views of the world gave Sam some real challenges. Fearing the world, Sam was constantly on guard:

"People are watching me. They are waiting to catch me in a weak moment so that they can take advantage of me. I have to be constantly on guard to make sure that they don't hurt me."

Sam's belief that other people were out to get him is an extreme example of how PWS perceive other people as always judging their blocking. Like Alan (Case Study 7, below), his motto was: "One must remain vigilant at all times lest someone take advantage of you or even kill you." Sam took that to extremes. I have frequently found similar though less extreme beliefs about the world in people who block (Figure 2.1).

"It is not OK to stutter."
"I fear being rejected."
"Others expect me to stutter."
"I feel hurt (not validated)."
"I don't measure up."
"I feel isolated from others."
"My life is out of control."
"I cannot speak."
"I am 'less than'."
"I look foolish."
"I am going to attract attention."
"People always judge me."
"I must conceal my emotions."
"What people say about me becomes truth."
"I must protect myself from being hurt by others."

"People judge the content of what I am saying."
"I will not let them see me struggle."
"I will not give others the chance to laugh at me."
"I will avoid situations that expose vulnerabilities."
"I must be right or people will judge me."
"I am scared of speaking in public."
"I need to be respected and loved to be fluent."
"People validate or determine my worth."
"I will not show my vulnerabilities."
"I must protect myself by not getting involved in relationships."

Figure 2.1: Beliefs about fearing what other people may think

Most PWS can usually identify with almost every one of these beliefs. The trouble is they do not entertain such beliefs one at a time. Instead, they keep adding them, layer upon layer, on top of their previous thoughts. Each time they imagine the often terrible

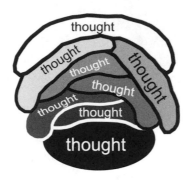

Figure 2.2: Layering thoughts

fear of what others may think of them because they block and stutter they build their "demon". Every time they think about this growing mass of negativity around their behavior, it gives it more substance. Not surprisingly, the PWS eventually comes to feel totally powerless to defeat their stuttering demon (Figure 2.2).

CASE STUDY 6

A PWS creates layers of negative thinking which lead to blocking. By unpeeling each layer and finding the core thought, the PWS has the opportunity for changing those limiting beliefs to ones which are more positive and supportive. For example, Sally created a web of negative and limiting beliefs of herself as a person. Here are some of the multiple layers of thoughts Sally was using to maintain her blocking (Figure 2.3). This had become embodied in her chest, neck, stomach and jaw.

"I am flawed."
"I am foolish."
"I am inadequate."
"I am a 'stutterer'."
"I am worthless."
"I am insecure."
"I am timid."
"I am anxious."
"I am tense."
"I am shamed."
"I am not enough."
"I pity myself."

"I am a poor performer."
"I am not a good communicator."
"I am an embarrassment."
"I don't want to look like a fool."
"I am frustrated with my life."
"I need protection from life."
"I need to change due to my
 stuttering."
"I am more sensitive."
"I can't handle criticism."
"I will not do anything that draws
 attention to myself."

Figure 2.3: Layers of beliefs

What happens to your state as you read through these two lists of negative frames? It is highly likely that you will find yourself going deeper and deeper into a negative state. The more you do "stinking thinking" the more of a "stinking state" you go into. How do you get out of this vicious spiral? One way is to think differently. If you are feeling down, *Stop!* right now, and get yourself back up into a good state for being curious about how to change your thinking.

You change how you think by changing your physiological state. Jump up and down, walk, run, play sport – anything that makes you feel good, happy, more alive, alert, and so on. Physical exercise changes your state. So right now, what could you do to make yourself feel really great and fully alive?

Remember: you are in control, you can choose to stop your debilitating thinking patterns. After all, you create the meaning of your experience. You know that you can change your mind by perceiving the world from a different point of view, to see the glass as half full, rather than half empty – by engaging in reframing. You examine your thoughts and then relabel them, reorganize them, reevaluate them, or even find them so ridiculous that you burst out laughing!

If thinking negative thoughts leads to blocking, then thinking positive thoughts can lead to fluency. Action follows thought. It makes a difference which kind of *content* you have in mind – and you are ideally positioned to decide that. However if thinking positively is not your usual pattern then you need to practice filling your mind with resourceful thoughts. A resource is anything that puts you in a good state, something you *apply* to a limiting situation in order to improve it. For example, in the present circumstances, a resource could be your ability to step back or disconnect from a debilitating mass of negative beliefs.

When the PWS *disconnects* from the negative web of thoughts and feelings attached to their blocking and stuttering they immediately become empowered and able to recover their fluency in speech. As a clinician, your goal is to get the PWS to disconnect from that debilitating web which they have been weaving since childhood. By disengaging the emotional attachments from their behaviors around speaking, they can adopt a more resourceful perception of themselves as worthy adults, no matter how they perform.

Using the maps of childhood

How often do people use their mental maps from childhood rather than updating them throughout their adult life? The PWS is metaphorically treating their childhood map as an accurate representation of the current situation. They are responding *now* to a trigger that has its origins way back in some traumatic childhood experience. In re-living that experience they respond as they did then by stuttering.

Alan (below) spent most of his long adult life living in a dysfunctional family in a state of constant fear of other people. As a consequence, he was unable to free himself from blocking and stuttering. The blocking was a direct result of that unconscious childhood learning. When he called particular people on the phone or spoke with them in public, in his mind he felt like a child and instantly behaved in a childlike manner. His out-of-date map told him it was time to be afraid once more. It makes sense, therefore, to ask the PWS how old they feel when they are in the blocking and stuttering state. They will be able to tell you, and they may surprise themselves when they realize how young they are acting!

CASE STUDY 7

One of my clients, Alan, has a business that involves renting out apartments and town houses. When he talks to a prospective tenant, he tends to panic and block. During my first telephone conversation with him he said:

"I have to produce. I have to produce. I have to rent these units. It is my responsibility. If I don't rent these units I will not have any income. I will become bankrupt. I will be *out in the streets*! Everything in my life is *out of control*!"

Alan has these immense fears even though he has adequate financial resources. In fact he doesn't have to continue working. Yet these fears are so ingrained that they override all adult reasoning.

Further inquiry revealed that he viewed his world as a place of immense competition. Alan's grandparents immigrated to the US from a country that had experienced tremendous horrors; his people had undergone persecution. Those fears had been passed down from generation to generation and were deeply embedded in him. Alan treats the world as a place to be feared. His motto is "One must remain vigilant at all times lest someone take advantage of you, and even kill you." In Alan's mind, everyone is out to get him.

To compound this, Alan grew up in a terribly dysfunctional family. His mother and father fought constantly. Alan's father came from a very violent family. As a younger man his father fought professionally, and this evolved into physically violence with both Alan and his brother. Consequently Alan developed the belief, "If I raise my hand, I will be slaughtered. I don't have any 'power'."

His father had also inculcated into Alan the belief that, "You have to get on *on your own* and *take care of business. You have to.*" Alan took this to mean, "I have no support and I must do it on my own." His dad taught him, "The door is wide going in and narrow coming out." By that he meant that it is easy to get in a bad situation but hard to get out of it. Coming from this domineering and violent father, Alan took these beliefs to heart. To Alan the world was not a friendly warm place, but a hostile enemy against which he had to constantly battle in order to survive.

Alan described his mother as "a very mean person." She was "always making fun of people and putting them down." As with all children, Alan personalized this by thinking, "If I do anything wrong, then I will be made fun of." Alan summarized his world: "I lived my life on edge, waiting for the other shoe to drop." He viewed his world as a mean, terrible, fearful and violent place that he was powerless to deal with.

If you take all those emotions that Alan experienced and embody them in the chest, throat and jaw – you have a block.

On one occasion Alan exclaimed, "The little kid (himself as a child) is getting back at his parents by being obstinate by stuttering. Everything else in my life is *out of control* so I will show them that I can control my speech by stuttering and they can't do anything about it. When I stutter, I embarrass them."

People who grow up in a violent, insecure, fearful, world, tend to generalize and assume that the entire world is similar to that one they grew up in. I have found that many PWS view the world as a place where "people are out to get them." Several of my clients have spoken with great fear about how "people are watching me to take advantage of me." To such people the world is an unfriendly place and they have few resources to deal with it. These beliefs usually spring from having a childhood like Alan's. Let me repeat that I have never worked with a PWS whose problems behind their fears did not originate in childhood – and that applies to mental-emotional problems in general.

Using outdated maps

Sam employs some beliefs about life which "support" his fearful behaviour. For example, that "Marriage is the end of love because it creates a miserable life" comes directly from his childhood experiences of his parent's fighting. When I provided him with a counter example of my wife and I who have been happily married for 38 years, he responded with his belief from childhood, "That is not 'real'." In other words, my "evidence" didn't count. It did not work because I wasn't speaking to an adult – I was speaking to a "temporary" child in an adult's body, and that child could not conceive of a happy marriage even one right in front of him. Operating off a childhood map fails to provide an accurate perception of the *present* reality that the person is living in.

How do we develop such limiting beliefs about our relationships with others? We know that they are learned and reinforced over time. As infants we are obviously totally dependent on caregivers to provide for our needs. In growing up we move from dependence to independence as we develop a richer sense of self. However, we need a secure foundation in order to mature into a healthy adult. In those early years we need a secure environment and must experience unconditional love by bonding with our parents. Without that, we grow up like Sally, feeling isolated and fearful of other people. Sally learned that adults were dangerous and were to be avoided. Thus she felt a need to be invisible. Had Sally had a loving and accepting mother, supported by a loving and supportive father, Sally would not have feared social settings so much. And Sally, in all likelihood, would not have grown up blocking. Remember that she embodied those negative emotions from the lack of bonding and unconditional love in her throat and jaw.

Meaning frames about self

If you have worked with PWS, you have probably frequently heard their beliefs about their blocking. Often the PWS is not consciously aware of the thought patterns that create that rich web of associations in their model of the world. One thought leads to another, and to another, and very soon the PWS is deeply enmeshed in a debilitating frame of meaning. For example:

> When I make a phone call I get nervous. When I get nervous I have the thought, "I bet I will block." Why do I always do this? Why can't I stop? I know I will block. I always have. Let me see. What do I need to say when I make that call? What words can I use that I won't block on …?

Having got this far, it is hard to turn back. But turn back they must. Your task is to find ways of intervening that will help them do that.

Being in control

PWS commonly say that they feel out of control with their speech. This contributes mightily to their fearing how others perceive them, because they certainly cannot control what other people think. The need to control is paramount to a person who blocks.

Here is Betty's story:

> My parents got divorced when I was six months old. I only saw my
> father on the weekends. He remarried, and his second wife had
> two children from her previous marriage. Her daughter was the
> same age as me. My stepmother hated me because I was a pretty
> little girl. She was incredibly sarcastic and nasty. I couldn't tell my
> father because "I had to please him and make him happy", and I
> didn't want to lose his love. Even when I visited him, he would
> ignore me and would leave me with "those people". I was full of
> shame, anger, sadness, fear and agitation. Later mom started meet-
> ing with a group of people and she left me alone. I was so alone.
> And then Mom became very critical of me ….

These statements are typical of the clients I work with. Needless to
say, such experiences are not conducive to creating a sense of
power and resourcefulness in one's life. Growing up in a family
where the environment is chaotic and unpredictable will in many
cases lead a person to believe they are powerless. They often grow
up without a sense of being in control. Sometimes people who put
a high value on control try to compensate by becoming control
freaks, wanting to control everything and everyone around them.
When they discover that the world cannot easily be controlled,
they then perceive the world as failing them (as their parents failed
them) and develop a sense of helplessness and powerlessness. The
more their control strategy fails to work, the more powerless and
helpless they feel.

In many cases, people who have been overwhelmed with pain in
childhood, and even adulthood, give control over to others. They
just tend to give up. Think of the statements in Figure 2.4 as
expressing a lack of personal control.

To reveal something about the childhood environment that led to
the creation of the beliefs that life was out of control and that they
must work to maintain control, ask the PWS: "How long has your
life been out of control?" "When did you first sense that you had
no control over your environment?"

If the PWS grew up in an environment that was safe, secure, and
that gradually allowed them to take more and more control over

"As a child my parents just ignored me."
"I was on the 'outside'."
"In school I never 'fit in'."
"I got teased a lot."
"I was never good enough."
"My parents wanted me to be perfect."
"I had to be seen, but not heard."
"I felt suffocated."
"My parents were constantly fighting, and I just used to hide in my room."
"My parents were ashamed of my stuttering."

"My parents were fast talkers.
"My parents insisted: 'you've got to get it out'."
"In my home showing emotions was a sign of weakness."
"My parents divorced when I was five years old."
"I only saw my dad on the weekends. He was a workaholic and was gone a lot."
"I always wanted to impress my dad so he would love me."

Figure 2.4: Beliefs about lack of personal control

their life, they will gladly answer positively. However, if security was under-represented during their early years, they probably cannot answer. Then you have to help them find examples of being in control despite those factors. There is usually some area of life in which they did have a sense of control, even if that meant rebelling against their parents in some way. They could self-harm, engage in drug-abuse or develop eating disorders. These could all be seen as expressions of "being in control of your own life". Alan used his stuttering as a means of getting back at his parents. He perceived that they were out of control so Alan chose to use stuttering to demonstrate that he could control his speech. It was a way for him to say, "I will show you I am not totally at your mercy."

Childhood is a time of confusing emotions anyway, but when the child is not listened to or taken seriously, it is hardly surprising that they turn inward and find other ways to deal with their emotions. Despite their best efforts they can never meets the needs of their parents or significant others, so they express themselves in the only way they can, and this may result in trying to control their own bodies and in inhibiting the muscles which control breathing and speech. These childhood patterns provide some kind of relief, but this continues and contributes to their blocking in later life.

Developing a sense of power and resourcefulness is absolutely essential in overcoming blocking. The psychologist Martin Seligman (1975, 1990) researched "Learned Helplessness" and "Learned Optimism". His work speaks clearly about how a person develops learned helplessness in becoming a victim of the blocking rather than taking control and becoming optimistic about overcoming the behaviour.

The 3Ps of learned helplessness

- **Personal:** People who block tend to personalize their disfluency. They tend to identify with the badness of their speech. "My speech is flawed, and so am I." It is as if the individual is thinking, "As I speak, so I am."

- **Pervasive:** The person generalizes from their disfluency in language and assumes that their flawed nature extends to other activities in their life. Everything in every part of their life must be bad.
  I hear many sad stories from people who block who have chosen not to go for advanced education; who spend hours studying a thesaurus to find substitute words for those they usually block on; who cannot ask someone out for a date; who do not apply for advancement at work, and so on, all because of how they speak on some occasions. It is heart-breaking to hear how this one issue can so permeate and determine someone's life.

- **Permanent:** After years of failed attempts at gaining fluency, many people come to believe that their stuttering will last forever. "I have done this since I was a child; I have tried everything; I have spent thousands of dollars ... and I still stutter." It is no wonder that they tend to develop a sense of helplessness about the problem.

One way of thinking about this is that when we make things **p**ersonal, let them **p**ervade other areas of our life and believe they are **p**ermanent, we *P* all over ourselves!

Learned optimism reverses these 3Ps

How can the PWS turn these three Ps around and look on the bright side? The first step is to have them notice that they are doing this, and then become curious about how exactly they are limiting their options. By mentally standing back they can observe themselves and make an honest appraisal of their behavior. There is no point in trying to pretend or to deny what they are doing. They need to adopt the attitude that they are responsible for their own behavior. "My body-mind knows how to speak fluently; I don't need to relearn how to talk. I can already do that. I just have to learn how to let go of the fear and anxiety that drives my blocking so that I can transfer my ability to speak fluently to all situations and contexts and I am going to do that."

- **Not Personal**: "I *accept* that I am more than my behavior. As a fully functioning human being I can take responsibility for what I do. And if I perform less than wonderfully in certain contexts then I can do something about that." Thinking in this way will affect everything you do.

- **Not Pervasive**: "I am widening my focus of attention, and *appreciate* all the other things in my life that I do well." "I am altering the way I talk about myself (to be more interested in other things) and I am in the process of doing that."

- **Not Permanent**: "When I look back at my life, I realize that I have always been making significant changes in who I am and what I do. Who knows what *awesome* changes I will be making in my speech in the future! I once learned to block and stutter and that means that I can unlearn them."

You are always "more"

Who are you? I mean, who are you *really*? This is an unanswerable question. Whatever description you put on yourself, you know that it does not adequately describe the rich complexity that you are. I love the statement, "No matter what you think you are, you are more than that."

If you are asked for a "self-definition" – when filling in a form, or writing a résumé – you adjust your definition to meet the needs of the person asking the question. You probably choose to label yourself in a way that communicates the essence of who you are to someone else: "I'm a therapist", "I'm a parent", "I'm single", or even, "I'm a stutterer". Each of these labels is based on a quality, on group membership, or on a particular behavior or thought pattern that you think encapsulates something of your nature. However, if you use derogatory terms or negative descriptions to put yourself down because there are aspects of yourself that you do not like, then how is that going to affect you as a person? (Perhaps I should stop using the term PWS and change it to PWUTS – People Who Used To Stutter, or even better, P – just People.) If you do notice you have slipped into this habit, simply remind yourself that, "True, at times I think of myself that way, but I am more than that." And then come up with an answer to: "What am I which is more than that …? And what am I that is *even more than* that …?" Continue as far as you like. Your unconscious mind will give you answers, so heed what comes.

As people mature into adulthood, they become increasingly self-aware, develop a richer concept of themselves as a person. Your sense of self is mostly maintained through the language you use – self-descriptions, labels, characteristics – together with some kind of evaluation: good or bad, desirable or undesirable, and so on. People update their self-understanding based on how they deal with the events in their lives, their interactions with others, and with the world in general. If what happens matches your expectations, you think you are doing well. If you are frustrated, you may think you are "hopeless" or "worthless". If you then feel contempt and despise yourself because your blocking and stuttering behavior led to unfulfilled expectations, then your model of the world may be perceived as letting you down as a human being.

A mature concept of self celebrates your sense of innate self-worth. PWS often view themselves as innately sick, as having little or no value and worth – just because they are human. Because they do typically view themselves as worthless, they tend to assume others have a low opinion of them too. They constantly seek the approval of others, hoping to discover that they are an OK person after all. But they keep on beating themselves up because of this awful blocking and stuttering behavior and because they feel so unworthy.

Countless times I have heard PWS belittle themselves, saying, "Bob, you must think I am weird." "Bob, I am sorry that I can't do better and be like your other clients. I know I am slow and stupid." Such statements break my heart for here I am talking to some of the bravest people with whom I have ever spoken to and they are constantly undervaluing themselves.

Creating a healthy view of self is an inside job. The clinician's aim is to assist the PWS in re-constructing their model of the world by including their bravery and persistence in dealing well with life's challenges. This is surely much better than having depressed areas on their map based on hurt and meanings from childhood. These people have survived in a world with a speech handicap, and have dealt with it through their own courage, strength, and determination. Because their model of the world already includes "speaking fluently" in some contexts, the clinician's job is to assist them in extending that ability to those parts which are still "depressed", and to ensure that they increasingly accept and appreciate themselves and not care whether they block and stutter.

Healthy people view themselves as innately valuable, worthwhile, lovable, and having dignity. They have nothing to prove, but everything to experience. They go about life exploring and enjoying those relationships and experiences that life offers. They do not let the judgment of others, much less the perceived judgments of others, affect them. Indeed, information from other people provides feedback on how they are doing as a human being, and which areas need their attention. Actually, once they reach that level of acceptance, most have already quit blocking and stuttering or have made major progress towards fluency.

To gain fluency, it is essential that a PWS learns how to apply one thought to another (see Exercise 3.5). When a person can access their resources at will, they can maintain state control, and maintaining state control is the key to overcoming blocking. Indeed, learning how to maintain state control is the key to much in life. The people who block whom I have assisted to become proficient at managing their own states in all contexts are able to transfer those states of fluency into contexts that formerly led to blocking.

Relationship with our thoughts

People sometimes develop poor relationships with their thoughts. If they are fearful about what something means, that affects how they respond to it, and creates a problem. Improving that relationship leads to overcoming the problem. In the present context, the PWS's relationship with their thoughts leads eventually to blocking. Ways to change your relationship with your thoughts was the subject of the ground-breaking work of Albert Ellis. Together with pioneer thinker Aaron Beck they are credited as being the fathers of Cognitive Psychology (of which NLP and Neuro-Semantics are branches). Ellis (1976) expounded his understanding of mind-body thus:

> Human thinking and emoting are not radically different processes; but at points significantly overlap. Emotions almost always stem directly from ideas, thoughts, attitudes, beliefs… and can usually be radically changed by modifying the thinking processes that keep creating them.

Ellis became renowned for his list of ten *Cognitive Distortions*. Cognitive Therapy aims to correct these cognitive distortions or faulty thought patterns – the type of thinking that frequently leads to depression (something many PWS suffer from on a regular basis; for them, "life is depressing"). Clinicians can benefit from a knowledge of this list of distorted thinking because the PWS usually demonstrates these distortions in their thinking. This list is based on Burns (1989):

1. **All or nothing thinking** – Another name for "black and white thinking". If your performance falls short of perfect, you see yourself as a total failure. This polarity thinking sorts the world of events and people in two extremes: good–bad, right–wrong, love–hate, and so on. Mapping the world in this fashion ignores the subtleties of life; the world has in-betweens, shades of gray. Failure to consider the middle zone can give rise to fundamentalism. The PWS exemplifies this by describing themselves in absolute terms: "I can't even talk. I am a total failure and always will be."

2. **Overgeneralization** – The PWS experiences a single negative event as a never-ending pattern of defeat. This behavior explains how those experiences in childhood (being pointed out, embarrassed, judged, abused and so on) continue into adulthood perceived as hopeless to change.

3. **Mental filter** – Concentrating so strongly on one aspect of a task or a situation to the exclusion of all else. The PWS becomes obsessive about trying to avoid blocking and stuttering.

4. **Disqualifying the positive** – The world is interpreted in a way that reinforces negative feelings and explains away positive ones. The PWS who is caught up in this is genuinely depressed about their blocking. They reject positive experiences by insisting they "don't count" for whatever reason, and maintain negative beliefs even though they are contradicted by everyday experiences. For instance, even though most PWS have consistently demonstrated fluency, many still hold to the belief that, "I have always blocked and stuttered and I always will." Their own fluency fails to convince them that blocking and stuttering is a learned behavior and that it can be unlearned.

5. **Jumping to conclusions** – Despite the lack of facts to substantiate their conclusion the PWS jumps to a negative interpretation. By their mind-reading shall you know them. As I have mentioned, PWS fear the judgments of others even when they do not know what is in the other person's mind. This generates unnecessary anticipatory fear which leads to further blocking and stuttering.

6. **Magnification and minimization** – PWS have a tendency to *Catastrophize* – entertain only "worst-case scenarios". This makes sense when you consider the worst-case scenario thinker learned this in childhood. With their childhood being filled with much pain, hurt and uncertainty, they come to expect bad things to happen and prepare themselves for it. They also *Awfulize* – always look on the dark side. Many PWS view their speech extremely negatively, and from there they *personalize* (see step 10) by identifying with this behavior.

7. **Emotional reasoning** – The PWS assumes their negative emotions necessarily reflect the way things are: "I feel it, therefore it must be true" or "I feel it and hence my blocking and stuttering is a physical problem." This type of thinking has led to the erroneous belief amongst speech pathologists that they need only treat the symptoms (the physical expression of blocking) rather than its cause (the mental frames that drive the blocking).

8. **"Should" statements** – Operating predominately by *necessity*, which escalates into *should*-ing *and must*-ing – which Ellis has humorously labeled "musterbation". Thinking the world *ought* to be a certain way puts pressure on the PWS: it generates unnecessary and inappropriate shame, guilt, self-contempt and other similar unresourceful states.

   PWS try to motivate themselves with *should*s and *ought*s, as though they must be punished before they can be expected to speak fluently. "I *ought* to be able to speak properly. After all, I am an adult. So I *must* stop this." As a consequence of continued blocking, they experience guilt. A common notion is the need to be "perfect". Rooted in childhood, this need drives *should*ing: "I *should* do better." "I *should* speak fluently." "I *must* be perfect or no one will like me." Obviously such thinking leads to more stress, more fear; more anxiety and consequently more blocking.

9. **Labeling and mislabeling** – This is an extreme form of overgeneralization. Instead of describing their blocking as a behavior that they do sometimes, they attach a negative label to themselves such as "I'm a loser." Such labeling leads to identifying with the behavior and that in turn tends to lock in the block. After all, if you believe yourself to be a loser then your life will be lived to prove that true.

10. **Personalizing and blame** – Is the PWS ever good at this! The PWS believes that they are the cause of their blocking and stuttering, which indicates that something is wrong with them as a person. Major problems may arise if the PWS's level of self-esteem is based on their speech and not on their innate worth as a human being. They judge their performance in terms of

whether or not they can please others by being fluent. Once the PWS learns that they are far more than their speech behavior, they are well on the way to fluency.

The way out of such cognitive distortions is to start thinking differently, and one way to do this is to consider the future in terms of what you want to have in it. The following section provides a systematic way of helping someone think positively about what they want.

Overcoming resistance

A tough realization of change is that when you *gain* something you also *lose* something. People sometimes resist change when the fear of loss is stronger than the desire for gain. Even though the PWS is keen to let go of a limiting behavior and can imagine how life will be better thereafter, they may still not change because there are still unresolved issues which need to be addressed first. It is as if there are "parts" of them which have objections (see Exercise 5.2, step 7).

PWS may resist overcoming stuttering because of the *secondary gain* they derive from it. It might seem crazy that someone would hang on to a debilitating behavior just because of the pay-off they get from it, but they do. The secondary gain may be getting protection or getting attention – benefits relevant to their childhood which they are hesitant to let go of. Until the mental frames which hold the blocking and stuttering in place are made conscious, and satisfactory alternatives found, they will continue to influence someone's behavior.

Imagining change as a magic wand which makes everything different could lead to uncritical and unrealistic expectations. When you think about your life, even when one big thing changed, many of the small things stayed pretty much the same. You still have to go shopping, pay the bills, put out the garbage. If the PWS suggests that, "Once I speak fluently everything will be wonderful", tactfully point out that it may not be as clear cut as that. Speaking fluently puts them on the same basis as other people. No longer are they "disadvantaged"; they will lose their "special status".

There are no longer any excuses for under-performing; they will simply need to use their talents more. It's a good idea to consider these losses and gains beforehand, so that they have more realistic expectations.

Language and your concept of self

How do negative concepts of self become so ingrained and so powerful that they can literally determine how a person speaks? It is because they seem real to the person. The word or label comes to stand for a whole array of experience which has been ignored or forgotten. For example, the words "flawed" and "broken" take on an aura of truth which seems inevitable. So how does this happen?

Language

Lives are dynamic, and experience can be perceived as a story or as a movie, possibly several movies at once. However, our language is far better suited to labeling *static* things: events, images, snapshots of our reality. Words tend to "fix" the world and our experience. Think about the words you use to describe a process or event which has been going on for some time: "my marriage", "my job" and so on. Words become a kind of shorthand way of referring to much larger stories or ongoing processes. Many concepts are labeled as if they are things – "relationship", "job" – when in fact they are ongoing processes – ways of *relating*, or *getting things done*. Unless you deliberately talk in terms of continuing change, most of the language you use refers to "what stays the same" in your mind. A similar thing happens in using adjectives to describe the qualities of something or someone. For example, describing them is "young" or "old" is imprecise and relative.

You use these verbal shortcuts all the time. They are neither good nor bad in themselves. If you didn't use them you would find it difficult to communicate; every conversation would take forever. However, it is when your communication is not working, when you are stuck with a fixed description of your reality, and you want to change, that is when the language itself needs to be investigated.

It can be hard putting your experiences into words. Much easier to use ready-made word forms or clichés for getting across what you want to say. But, as with every well-used term or phrase, they soon lose their power to inform, because other people *think* they know what you mean when in fact they do not. It's also probable that you think your description of yourself is accurate when in fact you are using imprecise tools. Everyday speech is usually inexact; it is "good enough" to the extent that the other person knows what to do as a result of understanding your communication. But when they are uncertain what you mean, or do not know how to respond, it is then that you need to become clearer in your use of language. You need to fill in the gaps, give examples, talk about movies rather than snapshots. So when another person says, "I am flawed", this kind of language is just the merest indication there is something they don't like about themselves. You don't know how precisely they think they are flawed, or what you are supposed to do about it. The person has somehow reduced a huge amount of information about themselves into one word, "flawed", and then *identified* themselves with this one word. If you want to intervene, then you must first recover some of the supporting thinking that led to the abbreviated description – because as it stands, there are no clues about how you could help them change anything.

Representing an action or process in terms of a single noun or adjective is called *nominalizing*. Nominalizations leave out a great deal of information: the single word "life" could represent a whole lifetime's experience; "worthless" or "foolish" (see Figure 2.3) are labels which the person applies to a complex cognitive analysis of behavior. This way of using language suggests how words both gain and lose meaning, and what we can do to change a particular meaning. "Stuttering" and "blocking" both refer to ongoing behaviors. By analysing the strategy the person is using for blocking or stuttering, what the person actually *does*, it becomes possible to change the strategy they use. They need to recover the "missing" information – the specific details of their strategy – in order to intervene and make adjustments.

Exercise 2.1: Recovering the evidence

Choose one of your favorite descriptions that you tend to believe about yourself. (You may identify with some of those in Figures 2.1, 2.3, 2.4 above). Now ask yourself these questions:

- How have I come to identify myself as *flawed*, *worthless*, *timid*, or whatever? What is the story behind that?
- What are the specific things that I *do* that I am defining in that very abbreviated way?
- What kind of movies am I making that define me as being flawed?
- How am I talking to myself so that I define myself as being flawed?

Answering these questions will begin to recover the story, the sequence of behaviors you engage in. By finding the meaning behind the words, the strategies and processes you use, you can then reorganize or edit them to produce you what you would rather have – fluency in speaking.

The words you use become associated with the feelings – they act as triggers for a particular state – and through habitual use get grooved into the muscles of your body. They feel real, and for some people, such feelings are the evidence for knowing something is real. The stronger this link between word/label and bodily feeling, the more challenging it is to alter.

Now we have another way of working: focusing on the words someone uses to talk about their experience. When a PWS tells you the way things are this provides an opportunity to find out how exactly they have constructed their model of the world. The good news is that it is always possible to undo the "realizing" process by examining the structure of the experience the words refer to. By bringing the strategies and stories into conscious awareness, it is possible to reorganize the strategies, to edit or rewrite the stories the PWS is using for knowing when to block and stutter.

You can also alter the meaning of – reframe – those contexts which they perceive as fear or anxiety producing. How you change the meaning of a limiting behavior, and how you re-create a model of the world so that it serve you better is covered in the remaining chapters.

Chapter Three

Changing Points of View

The nature of communication

Given that blocking has a cognitive component, then we can begin to explore ways of changing that blocking behavior by changing the way the PWS communicates.

Why do you communicate to others? This is not a trick question. The answer is that essentially you communicate to other people because you want them to do something. You establish an outcome or intention which involves them changing in some way, and then do whatever is necessary to try to achieve that. Even in the most friendly, laid-back situations, you want other people to listen to your stories and respond to them. There is a huge difference between communicating to another person, and talking to the furniture; in the former case, you expect some kind of response.

You communicate because you want to change the world in some way. Therefore it helps to be clear about what exactly it is that you want to happen, what exactly it is you want to be different. That is why this chapter covers creating *well-formed outcomes*, because every act of communication implies some kind of purpose or outcome.

An over-riding concern for the PWS is to be fluent. But not always. They may say that they want to be comfortable with themselves even though they stutter. I hear this a lot: "Bob, just get me to where I stop beating myself up because I stutter." "Just get me to where I am OK with myself and not so overly anxious because I stutter." These people seem to know that once they get to where they are comfortable with themselves even though they stutter, the main issues are resolved. Their conversational outcome is the same as with "normal" people.

There is a saying: "You get what you concentrate on." If you think about the horrible things that could happen to you … well, you know what? They do. Therefore part of the changing of your behavior is changing the content of your thoughts. This means paying attention to what comes to the forefront of your mind, and noticing whether you are counting your blessings or on the look-out for disasters, threats, or someone to blame!

What is your point of view?

Most people make movies in their mind when they think about what they do. Recall what you did when you got up this morning. Most people remember past events as if they are watching movies of what happened – though obviously these mental movies have different qualities from looking at the world in the here and now.

There are some interesting variations in the way people see their movies. One significant difference is:

- You are actually *in* the movie, looking out through your eyes at what is happening around you.
- You can *see yourself* acting in the movie. It is as though you are in a cinema watching everything that is happening at a distance on the screen.

Of course, you may use both of these points of view at different times, but you probably have a preference. You may be able to switch from one mode to the other easily at will. This distinction is important, because in the first case, the *associated* version, you are also strongly connected to your emotions. Your mind does not really distinguish between something happening "for real" and your remembered version of it. If you are associated in the memory, it can still have an emotional impact. Experience this for yourself:

- Recall a mildly unpleasant memory. If you see yourself in that memory – *dissociated* – then deliberately associate into the memory and notice if your feelings increase.

Most people recall painful memories as associated, but not everyone. Some only associate into those memories that are extremely painful.

Exercise 3.1: The lemon

Try this:

Imagine opening the door of your refrigerator and taking out a lemon. Close the door, take a knife, put the lemon on the cutting board. Slice the lemon into halves, and then into quarters. Pick up one of the quarters and put that slice of lemon into your mouth. Squeeze it and feel the lemon juice squirting into your mouth. Are you salivating yet?

Most people find an increase in salivation. This simple experiment illustrates how the mind does not differentiate between real and imaginary experiences.

On the other hand, if you were watching a movie of yourself doing that, it is highly likely that your response would not be as strong. When you are observing what happened from the outside, from a *dissociated* position, you are usually more objective and not connecting with those feelings in the same way. You can evaluate your experience and have feelings about it, but you are not going to be so caught up in them as when you are associated. This associated/dissociated distinction is important in some of the exercises and processes that follow.

When you switch from an associated memory to a dissociated one, note how your feelings diminish when you dissociate from the memory and see yourself in it.

Focus of attention

Whether or not someone blocks depends on how they perceive the situation they are in. Another distinction looks at what specifically they are paying attention to in the *content* of the movie. For situations perceived as threatening, PWS have programmed themselves to experience a state of fear or anxiety. In non-threatening situations they are happy to interact with the other person and able to focus on their individual or joint objectives. For example, one of my clients told me, "When I am by myself, I can't even make myself stutter; but as soon as I walk out that door and speak to anyone, I almost always block and stutter." Another said, "When I speak to someone that I know and feel safe with, I do not stutter. When I speak to someone whom I do not know I feel unsafe and I always block and stutter."

Obviously, during those times of fluency, the object of their attention is quite different from what they are paying attention to when they block and stutter. Therefore it is important to ask the PWS: "Where are your thoughts directed when you are blocking; where are they directed when you are fluent?" You are eliciting what they have in focus, what is in the *foreground* of their attention.

People tend to block when they focus exclusively on themselves and their present experience of fear and anxiety. Instead of attending to the other person with whom they are communicating and the content of what they are saying, they focus on their fear of stuttering, and that fear grabs their total attention; they cut off from the other person and the communication ceases. Their emotional states come into the foreground – and no one's needs are met because these people are unable to communicate effectively.

A PWS may say, "Now wait a minute Bob. It is not *myself* that I am focusing on; I am focusing on the other person and how they will judge my speech." However, that judgment is actually theirs. They are hallucinating what the other person is thinking about them, imagining being judged by that other person. It is as if the PWS is observing what is happening from an observer position (see below): monitoring their own *performance* rather than holding in mind the *purpose* of the communication, and this kind of detached awareness interferes with their functioning.

On the other hand, when speaking fluently, the person is focusing on their outcomes for the conversation, what they want to happen. They are not even bothering to think about any imagined judgments; any fear of blocking and stuttering is irrelevant. Think of a time when you were busily engaged in doing something you love

– a hobby or sport, for example. You are so intent on what you are doing, giving it your all, concentrating on achieving perfection, that if someone asks "Are you happy?" you have to detach yourself and think about it. You are happy, but you only realise this after you stop to consider. In the same way, when you are fluent, you are not thinking about fluency, because you are busy getting on with living and communicating. You only have time for the fears when you stop interacting.

In mind-reading what the other person is thinking, the PWS creates a story which inevitably leads to an unhappy ending: their status is lowered in the eyes of the other person, they think they are inadequate, to be pitied, and so on. This story dominates their thinking. The story then feeds back on itself – no facts or evidence from the outside are required! – and the fears and anxieties multiply to the extent that the only object of attention is the fear itself. That then becomes a self-fulfilling prophecy: the muscles oblige, the blocking occurs, the person stutters. If however the PWS focuses on an external outcome, such as getting the other person to do something, their muscles will adjust to help them achieve that.

The reason I ask clients to practice going in and out of the states of fluency and blocking is to teach the PWS behavioral flexibility. They are already familiar with each state; what they need is the facility for changing their states. No one lives their entire life blocking. Therefore they need to identify the strategy they already use to do this, streamline it, and practice it so that they can get out of the blocking state into another state whenever they want. It is simple, yet profound. Therefore, you need to help them find out exactly how they do this. Ask, "How do you do that?" "How does your focus change?" "How do you talk to yourself differently?" "How do you give yourself permission to be fluent?" Take note of the answers as they will provide you with information you can use in assisting them to alter their states at will. The more they practice moving from one state to another, the better they will be at reducing the power of the old blocking strategy. They are training their mind to choose which state they want to be in.

Focus of attention

Effective communication requires that you pay attention to the other party. Therefore, instead of watching themselves or engaging in mind-reading, they need to concentrate on what they want to achieve.

Exercise 3.2: Where is the focus?

This exercise assists the PWS to become aware of the difference between where they focus when blocking and stuttering, and where they focus when fluent.

It also provides practice in switching the focus of attention from internal to external, from judging their performance to focusing on their outcomes. In my experience this takes time and plenty of practice. Once you know the PWS can switch states successfully, ask them to notice what they bring into the foreground in each state.

Access a recent state of blocking
- While you are thinking about that state, notice what you are paying attention to. What is in primary focus while you block?
- What is your intention or purpose in this context?
- Given what you are focusing on, can you identify what actually triggers the fear of blocking?

Access a recent state of fluency
- While you are thinking about that state of fluency, notice what you are paying attention to. Where or on what are you focusing?
- What is your intention or objective in this context?

Developing a Well-formed Outcome for fluency

When the PWS chooses to move from blocking/stuttering to freedom/fluency, they must clearly know what they want and have the commitment to achieve it. This often requires a tremendous shift in the meanings they give to their speaking. In your clinician role,

I encourage you to maintain your outcome focus by holding in your mind the agreed upon outcome that your PWS clients assert.

The NLP Well-Formed Outcome process is an extremely effective and practical tool for bringing a specified outcome into the *foreground* of attention. A well-formed outcome is one that the PWS devises and which is framed in a way that makes it more likely to be achieved.

Exercise 3.3: Outcome setting

The PWS's internal and external dialogs provide clues on what needs to change. There are examples of the way PWS talk to themselves and to others throughout this book. People who are stuck tend to focus more on defining the problem rather than on finding solutions. This outcome-setting exercise gets the PWS thinking differently: what they want instead rather than what they want to get rid of, what they *do* want, rather than what they don't want. It also enables you to assist the PWS in identifying how they will get it. At each step the PWS thinks about the ecology of each proposal, to check that the outcome is right or appropriate for them.

Overview
1. State the outcome in positive terms.
2. State the outcome in sensory terms.
3. State your outcome in a way that is compelling.
4. Quality control your outcome.
5. Take personal control
6. State the context of your outcome.
7. State the resources you need for your outcome.
8. Future pace – check that it works.

Although the PWS can use this model on their own, I recommend that you first ask them the questions so that they can focus on finding the answers.

1. **State the outcome in positive terms.**
   Describe the present situation and compare it with the desired future outcome.
   • What do you want? What do you want to do differently?
   • Where are you now?

- Where do you want to be?
- What are you going toward?

Make sure that the PWS is able to state what they want to be able to do in positive language. For example, if they say they want to "stop stuttering" have them turn this around so that they are focusing on "becoming fluent".

In Case Study 1 in Chapter One, Susan stated a number of beliefs about herself which suggested a rather negative outlook. Figure 3.1 shows some positive reframes of those negative beliefs.

I am *not* ...	Positive reframe:
broken ...	I am whole.
inadequate ...	I am sufficient.
shy ...	I am able to deal with people on my own terms.
anxious ...	I feel the adrenalin rush that will allow me to ...
foolish ...	I learn from my mistakes.
worthless ...	I am a valuable member of society.
ashamed ...	I learn from my mistake.
angry ...	I get fired up so that I change things.
abnormal ...	I am unique.

Figure 3.1: Beliefs about self

2. **State the outcome in sensory-based terms.**
   The more realistic their story of the future behavior, the more likely it is to happen. Have the PWS envisage their outcome in terms of a movie in which they can see themselves speaking fluently in a number of situations which in the past were problematic.

   - What sequence of steps or stages is involved in reaching this outcome?
   - How will you break your outcome down into small enough chunks so that each is do-able?
   - How will you know that you have achieved your outcome? What will you see, hear and feel when you have it?

3. **State the outcome in a way that you find compelling.**
   People only achieve their goals when they are motivated, so find out the PWS's level of motivation:

   - How compelling is your outcome?

You can tell from the way they talk about their outcome whether they are inspired or not. If they seem unenthusiastic, help them make their outcome more compelling by asking them:

•   What else needs to be there for you to really want this?

Make sure that they imagine getting their outcome in a dissociated fashion – they can see themselves in the movie.

4. **Run a quality control check on the outcome to make sure it is appropriate.**
    •   Is the desired outcome right for you in all circumstances of your life?
    •   Is your outcome appropriate in all your personal relationships?
    •   What will having your outcome give you that you do not now have?
    •   What will having your outcome cause you to lose?
    •   Is your outcome achievable?
    •   Does it respect your health, primary relationships, and so on?

Often when people set outcomes, they only focus on the positive gains of their desire, and fail to consider what they will inevitably lose. All change involves gains and losses, and these need to be thought about at an early stage, to avoid later "disappointments". These four questions (Figure 3.2) cover all contingencies:

•   What will happen if you get your outcome?
•   What will happen if you do not get your outcome?
•   What will not happen if you get your outcome?
•   What will not happen if you do not get your outcome?

	Does not happen	Happens
Get outcome	What will not happen if you get your outcome?	What will happen if you get your outcome?
Not get outcome	What will not happen if you do not get your outcome?	What will happen if you do not get your outcome?

Figure 3.2: Cartesian contingencies

- Run a quality check to make sure that your outcome fits every part. Ask, "Are there parts of me that objects to actualizing this desired outcome?" If so, address those concerns (see Exercise 5.2, step 7).
- Pay attention to how your whole self responds to the question in terms of images, sounds, words, and sensations within you.

Considering the consequences ...

I emailed a question to one of my clients who blocks: "What would happen if you *didn't* have fear and anxiety about blocking?" My intention was to get him to consider some alternatives which would change his way of thinking about his blocking by considering alternatives. This client used his work to hide from facing himself and other people. One answer he gave was that he would have interests other than his work. In his email he also listed the following:

- I would be confident.
- I would be centered.
- I would be an equal to others.
- I would be more of a risk taker, more adventuresome.
- I would be positive instead of cynical.
- I would stop taking responsibility for other people's actions, but still feel compassion for them.
- I would feel the presence of God in my life on a consistent basis.
- I would be joyful and loving.
- I would know that however it turns out, it's fine as long as I gave it my best effort.
- I would be excited about lots of stuff.
- I would give more time to those people who care and love me.
- I would be non-judgmental and more understanding.
- I would have close friends.
- I would be accepting of myself without worrying what other people think or what they would do to me.

Wow! Look at all those outcomes which are inhibited by their fear and anxiety around stuttering. This typical response illustrates just how important it is to consider what has been put in the background because of some limiting perception and behavior.

5. **Take personal control.**
   Next check that the PWS has an effective strategy for achieving their outcome.

   - Is achieving this within your power or ability to do?
   - What is the first step? Can *you* take this first step?
   - Are you able to deal with whatever happens during the process?

6. **State the context of the outcome.**
   The PWS needs to identify which contexts are the problem ones. They may think of them in terms of the particular people or the kind of people they encounter, or it could be specific locations. They need to have their outcome generalized so that it will meet all possible situations in the future.

   - Where, when, how, and with whom, will you apply this outcome?

7. **State the resources needed to achieve the outcome.**
   Resources can be states and strategies that allow for fluent speaking.

   - What resources will you need in order to get this outcome?
   - Who will you have to become?
   - Who else has achieved this outcome?
   - Have you ever had or done this before?
   - Do you know anyone who has?

8. **Future pace – check that it works.**
   When the outcome has been stated to the PWS's satisfaction, have them run the movie and see themselves in the future with that outcome already achieved. From observing this image or movie, consider:

   - How will you know that your outcome has been realized?
   - What will let you know that you have attained that desired state?
   - Are there any adjustments you would like to make to make this even better?

Foreground/background – qualities that make a powerful difference

This exercise has its foundation in Gestalt Psychology. The purpose of the exercise is to assist the PWS in being able to foreground their intention in communicating and background those fears that block communication.

Exercise 3.4: Changing foreground and background

Overview

1. Think of the next time you will likely block.
2. Freeze the movie and locate the picture.
3. Step back and look beyond the picture of the block and see the resources in the background.

1. Ask the PWS to think of the next time they are likely to block. In all probability, they will create a picture of the person in the particular context.

2. Ask them to freeze the movie, and to notice where in reference to their eyes do they see that other person in their context. Is that picture in front of them? Is it down or up, to the right or to the left? In all likelihood that picture will be right in front of them and it is the only thing they are looking at.

3. Now ask them, "What are you *not* seeing?" What? Notice what you are not noticing? Yes, that is exactly what you want them to pay attention to: what in that picture they are *not* seeing. Because they are so focused on that person and the particular context which they are afraid will trigger their blocking they do not see anything else. Ask them to step back from that image to get a different perspective on it. From this position ask them to notice what they can see behind the first image. What is beside it and beyond it? What else is out there that they were not seeing at first?

Focusing on something to the exclusion of everything else is called *foveal* vision. In order to step back, you engage your *peripheral*

Figure 3.3: Alternating frames
(Based on 'My Wife and My Mother-in-law' by cartoonist W.E. Hill, published in *Puck* in 1915.)

vision. So step back, be aware of your peripheral vision and see everything around that original image. Not only look to each side, but look to see what is *behind* the picture of the block. Allow your awareness to go *beyond* the image of the block. What is *back there*?

In every picture, image, and movie that you are seeing, some things are in the foreground and other things are in the background. When we foreground *problems* they become bigger and more challenging. When we foreground *resources* we become more skilled, competent and bold.

What do you see when you look at the picture in Figure 3.3? An old woman or a beautiful young lady? If one of these answers surprises you, look again.

(Hint: The old woman's nose is the young girl's chin. You need to foreground the young woman's nose in order to see her. In doing so, you background the old woman, changing the bump on the old woman's nose to the young woman's complete nose. To see the old woman, foreground the young woman's necklace and perceive it as the old woman's mouth.)

You see *either* the old woman *or* the young woman. You can't see both simultaneously. It's similar to the way fluency and fear are competing concepts. If what is in the foreground does you no favors, why not put that in the background and replace it with something more useful? Once you are aware that you have a choice, you can see which you want to see. When it comes to blocking or stuttering, knowing that both options are available to you, which do you want to see in the foreground of your movies?

Consider the PWS who had an image of himself as a scared little kid who froze in the presence of authority figures. When he froze he blocked. He had another image of himself as a resourceful adult who always spoke fluently. When he saw the scared little kid, guess where the adult was? The scared little kid was in the foreground and the mature fluent adult was in the background.

Foregrounding resources

What resource states would help you foreground your behaviour of choice? Which resources would enhance your performance as you go on stage in the theater of your mind? You choose. Because you have already experienced states such as faith, courage, relaxation, presence of mind, feeling centered, being whole and so on, that means that you can have activate them as resources whenever you want them.

CASE STUDY 8

Jack provides us with an example of acceptance:

Jack told me during a phone consultation that before he called me he was becoming anxious about the call. He was worried that I would be thinking that he should be further along with the fluency then he was. So, again, we hear a person who blocks worried about what the other person may or may not be thinking about his or her speech.

By the way, people who block do not have a monopoly with such thinking. The PWS should take heart as they have a lot of company in the so-called "normal" world. Caring too much about what others think is very common. It is a part of being human – we probably all do it to some degree. During childhood we learn how the world works and that includes predicting what other people are going to do. And we are often expected to be a certain way for our parents or our teachers. However, we can never achieve "perfection". This is also part of being human, because if we were perfect we would never learn anything worth knowing about ourselves.

Jack told me that in some areas he was much more fluent. And that when he did stutter that wasn't as important to him as before. He was coming to the point where he was giving himself permission to stutter without feeling bad about himself. Indeed, he said, "It is really not blocking; it is more stumbling."

Here we have an example of how speech improves once the person accepts their experience and then relabels or reframes it.

However, he said, in some contexts he works up a lot of anxiety over an upcoming conversation with others. It happened as he thought about talking with me this morning. Jack was imagining what I would be "expecting" from him as a result of our therapy and his fear that he was not delivering, because in some contexts he was still blocking and stuttering.

So he is still running a movie which predicts what is going to happen – and that easily becomes self-fulfilling.

Jack went on to explain that he is able in some contexts to reframe this problem, but in others, as with me, he hasn't been able to change this. I asked him how he was doing it in other situations. He said that he could reframe away those old fears with the thoughts:

- "I give myself permission to be vulnerable."
- "I give myself permission to be who I am and not to think about other people's feelings. I can do this and not be selfish."
- "I am not going to guess what other people may or may not be thinking about me and *deprive them of knowing who I am*." (This one is a powerful reframe for him.)

We had uncovered these resource states in earlier sessions and they are proving most helpful. Desiring to build on these resource states and to apply them to the problem at hand about his fearing my expectations of him, I asked him *how* he was able to apply the above frames of mind to the old fears, because knowing *how* to do something is often more important than knowing what to do.

Jack explained that he would have a picture that represented the resource state right out in front of him. Then he would place a visual picture that represented the problem state behind the picture of the resource state. He would then bring the picture of the problem state up and into (and sometimes through) the resource state. Using this procedure he could:

- see the problem state through the eyes of the resource state and reframe it.
- mesh the two together, resulting in a reframe.
- totally reframe the problem state away.

What was happening in the situation with me? The picture of his anticipatory anxiety of not meeting my expectations was of the two of us together and him saying to himself, "Bob will think I should be further along than I am." "Bob has helped others quicker than he has helped me." "I am not progressing fast enough."

Does this sound familiar? That is how you work up a good state of anticipatory anxiety that once it is embodied in your gut, torso, throat and jaw as with my client, you have a full fledged block.

When he brought that image forward and meshed it with his resource image, the meaning totally changed. He said, "It's just two guys talking." And his speech? He was fluent, perfectly fluent. At the beginning of our session he was having difficulty speaking: stuttering quite a bit but not really blocking. By the end of the session he was totally fluent.

Jack will be taking today's learning and will practice installing it much deeper. As you know, it is one thing to speak fluently with your therapist; it is another to speak fluently with your peers.

Exercise 3.5: Applying resources to your thinking

This is the way Jack was thinking about his expectations (you may do it differently).

Overview

1. Access a resourceful thoughts that are powerful enough to over-whelm the fear of blocking.
2. Look into your gallery of pictures and note the qualities of each one of your thoughts: fear, faith, courage, and so on.
3. Expand your resourceful images so that they completely cover the negative images of fear.

1. Consider the fear-ridden thought that you will block and then stutter. Make it a static image. Now access resourceful thoughts about having faith or courage. What do you have faith in? What are you courageous about? Allow your mind to produce images to represent several different states. Label each image as it arrives, "fear", "faith", "courage" and so on, and put it at some distance, so that you can see them all together, rather like pictures on the wall of an art gallery.

2. Look at your gallery, and notice how you have represented each thought. What does the thought of "fear" look like? What does "courage" look like? How do you represent "faith"? You may have static images, or movies. You will probably notice that these images vary in brightness, color, size, and so on, and that maybe the positive thoughts are bigger and brighter than the negative ones. These are usually the kinds of distinctions our minds make in representing such ideas.

3. Still looking at your set of images in front of you, in your mind, begin to expand the positive ones, the "faith" and "courage" (and any more you think would be useful to have) and make those images bigger so that they completely cover the negative image of "fear".

In metaphorical terms, "the good guys win" – if you allow them to. So just relax, notice these changes going on in front of you as you allow your positive resources to dominate your thoughts.

Where is that old negative thought now? Somewhere way in the background. In the foreground you have the resources of faith, courage, and so on. You have taken the thoughts of faith and courage and applied them generously to your general way of being.

When you bring your resources to bear on the fear of blocking, the positives win out every time, just so long as you allow that to happen. Finally, bring these positive resources back into your body. Find a way of reintegrating this way of perceiving the world into your body. For example, you could use your hands to bring these resources into your heart area.

Exercise 3.6: Foregrounding resources

This exercise asks the PWS to look for resources that are in the background of the "fearful and anxious" sensory-rich movie of their blocking. By doing this, the PWS becomes better at controlling their mind-body state.

Overview

1. Step back from your movie and step into a dispassionate state of critical analysis.
2. Access a state of fearing that you will block. Step into that state of fear by imagining yourself in the context where you would have this fear.
3. From the background of your mind access a strong resourceful state of courage, faith, determination, and so on. Amplify it by making the movie vivid and using empowering language.
4. Apply your resource state(s) to the fear of blocking. Do this using language or any combination of visual, auditory, or kinesthetic resources.

Before teaching others how to do this, you need to do it on yourself and understand how you did it. Think of something you are fearful or anxious about, such public speaking, and run the pattern on yourself.

1. First make sure the PWS is in a good state. Then have them mentally step back so that they are able to examine the movie they make dispassionately.

2. Ask them to recall a time when they were blocking and fearful, and watch that movie from a safe position. Say "Remember a time when you were blocking. What are you paying attention to?" Usually they will be totally focused on themselves or on the other

person, mindreading them like mad, that they will not be seeing anything else at all clearly.

Then ask, "How close are you to the other person?" Ask them to mentally step back so that they can see more of the area behind and beside the image that represents blocking, and to pay close attention to what they have not been seeing. Ask, "What is there that you are not seeing?"

3.   Now, ask them to look *behind that* or *beyond that* and notice the resources *back there.* Say something like, "Yes, those resources are within you and you can be aware of them if you just pay attention. You may experience these resources as behind you, or supporting you in some way. At the moment they may be quite distant, far behind you in the background and you are only just aware of them. Or you may experience the resources you need actually inside yourself, maybe a feeling, maybe a sense of being bigger, more confident, so that having these resources, you hear yourself speaking confidently and fluently with that other person. You may think of these resources as *confidence, calmness, courage* or *faith.*" Amplify these resource states as needed.

4.   Once the PWS understands the model, has the fear fore-grounded, and is aware of the resources behind and beyond the fear, say, "As you become more aware of the resources that are available to you, you can allow them to become stronger, closer, with you and within you. And as you bring those resources into the foreground of your mind just push that old fear of stuttering way into the background. You may wish to just let it go so far that it either disappears, dissolves or explodes." To make this even more powerful, do what Jack did and allow the resource state to do whatever it wants in order to remove or destroy the problem state.

Practice finding different resources, applying them to the unre-sourceful movie, and notice which have the greatest effect. Jack uses pictures; I do it using words. I visualize the word "fear" and above that I put the word "faith." Behind that visual of the word "faith" is a picture of Jesus who, for me, empowers the word "faith." I then move the visual of the word "faith" down on top of the word "fear" and the word "fear" breaks into a thousand pieces. Others do it kinesthetically as they will move the feeling of courage and/or faith into the location of the feeling of fear. When you have "courageous" fear or "faithful" fear, how does that change the fear?

Applying resources to completely cover the negative image of fear, usually results in a shift in thinking. When Jack brought his image of fear forward and melded it with his resource image "the meaning totally changed". How the PWS applies their resources is up to them. They can do it slowly and gradually and see the old fears and anxieties fading into the background, or suddenly and completely and experience a dramatic change in how they are.

Note: A person with religious beliefs may discover the presence of God. Yes, resources flow from God into them, just so long as they allow themselves to stand far enough back from that debilitating situation. In the next section we will discuss further how to lead the PWS in accessing their higher spiritual resources.

Meta-stating

Everyone has the ability to access resources that will change the way they are at any one time, and can deliberately choose to apply them to any situation. If, for example, the PWS only applies a state of courage when thinking about speaking to a friend then they can learn to apply it to strangers as well. It is the state of mind, and not the content of the state, that makes the difference.

Exercise 3.7: Basic meta-stating

The previous pattern is an example of what its originator, L. Michael Hall calls Meta-stating – the process of applying resources to debilitating states (Hall, 1996, 2000, p. 47). The essence of this way of changing is:

1. Access a state which is limiting or debilitating, such as the fear of blocking.
2. Think of an appropriate resource which when you *apply* it to the fear of blocking will minimize the fear.
3. Associate into that resource state. Start by recalling a time when you had this state before, and then allow it to become stronger to completely fill you.

4. Staying in this resourceful state, *apply* it to the fear of blocking. Allow the resource state to envelop and permeate that fear of blocking, so that it dissolves and loses its power.
5. This change in your state can remain with you and continue to influence the way you are in the world. Still in this new state imagine yourself going through the rest of today, tomorrow, next week and the months to come, and experience life with a state of resourcefulness.

Because the fear has been well learned, it may take several repetitions of applying your resources over a period of time for your fear of blocking to diminish and eventually go away. Practice is essential. Every time the fear of blocking comes up, apply your resource state to the fear. Eventually the fear will weaken and disappear.

When the triggers for the fear are present your mind-body used to immediately respond with fear. Every time you challenge this connection you are interrupting the old strategy and in effect saying "No" to the fear and "Yes" to your resource state (see Exercise 6.3).

This meta-stating exercise involves changing the way you perceive your fear. You put yourself in a position of relative power, and use the positive energy of your resources to overcome the limitations of the unwanted state.

Changing your point of view – perceptual positions

You are constantly changing your point of view, altering the way you perceive and understand your experience. In fact, every process in this book gets you to do this, because change entails perceiving your reality in a significantly different way. Although there are infinite different points of view, they can be categorized into five distinct *perceptual positions*. Each has a particular function and thus provides an alternative way of understanding what is happening. This section is about how you can move at will through the five perceptual positions in order to create the changes you want.

The fear relating to blocking comes from the point of view that the world is fixed in some aspect, that there is nothing to be done to change things. PWS get stuck in this point of view, and cannot conceive of alternatives being possible. There is a way out: imagine *stepping outside* those fears around blocking and stuttering and adopting a point of view in which change is possible, a position which enables fluent speech. For example, you feel confident and know that you can achieve great things by pretending you are an expert. That's a change of point of view that the PWS can make to deal with their fear.

Deliberately changing your point of view is both useful in that it allows you to engage with the world in a different way, and provides a general strategy for dealing with any kind of change. It increases your mental flexibility in the way you perceive the world and thus in how you make meaning of the people and events you encounter.

The realization that humans operate from five basic ways of looking at experience offers tremendous potential in managing your own states and enhancing your communication. NLP's original three positions have now been expanded to five (see Young 2004, and Figure 3.4), and these are simply numbered first, second, third, fourth and fifth perceptual positions respectively. You

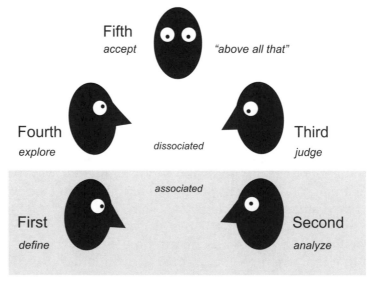

Figure 3.4: Perceptual positions

already use these perceptual positions; this model provides a way of thinking about them and using them systematically. Here we will consider how they work for people who block. As a clinician it is important that you recognize how to move flexibly around these different positions yourself in order to benefit from the insights offered by each perceptual position.

Associated points of view

First and second positions are both associated – you are fully in the experience. When you are fully associated in a memory, it is as if you are looking out through your eyes, hearing the sounds and feeling the feelings, and therefore you do not see yourself in the picture.

First position

This is the familiar position of being in your own body, looking out at the world from the viewpoint of being yourself. It's ego-centric – the normal and healthy position of seeing, hearing, and feeling from inside your self. It's your truth, your immediate needs that matter, and you take less account of anyone else's position. You simply think, "How does this conversation or communication affect me?" In first position you speak with authenticity, you present yourself, your thoughts, feelings, and responses congruently. You disclose, listen, inquire, and are present for others.

The down-side of first position is that you get stuck: the PWS is totally blocked. The solution is to move to another perceptual position and view their blocking from a different perspective. Although this kind of shift may require some effort, it liberates the PWS and enables them to gain fluency. Now it is not the case that they have never done this before. They have – but they need to learn how to do it in the blocking context.

Second position

Second position offers alternatives. One aspect of this is pretending to be another person, imagining how everything appears from their physical location. You put yourself in a different context: in the other person's body, looking at the world – and at yourself – through their eyes. "As this other person, what do I see, hear, and feel in this relationship, this communication?"

Experiencing how someone else perceives a situation provides you with empathic understanding. Although this is your imagination, the remarkable thing is that the more exactly you copy how the other person is, in terms of body, mind and spirit, the closer you come to experiencing things as they do, to seeing things from their point of view.

In everyday life you may wonder, "Now, what would he or she do in this situation?" Only by temporarily becoming that other person can you begin to find out. Adopting second position is important when you need flexibility in dealing with someone else, especially if there is any conflict.

When you find yourself thinking about someone's point of view *objectively*, then you have moved to third position. It is easy for the PWS to get into trouble here. They think "If I were in your shoes …" but instead of empathizing with them they mind-read them as judging the PWS's stuttering. Sometimes the PWS in second position looks back at themselves in first, sees their facial contortions and so on, and that jumps them back into the first position and ratchets up their emotional state.

The dissociated points of view

Third and fourth positions are dissociated: you are thinking *about* experience. If you recall a memory and see the whole thing, including yourself, as if from a fly-on-the-wall position, or as if you are watching a movie in your mind, then that memory is dissociated.

Being dissociated from an experience you can act more objectively because you are not involved in those events in the same way. There are two essentially different dissociated points of view: third and fourth positions. These positions are about interpreting and responding to what is happening. In third position you are evaluating or judging the entire event or conversation. This invokes your system of values, and moral outlook. In fourth position you observe, witness, and explore the situation in terms of metaphors, connections, ramifications and possible consequences.

Third position

Third position is about evaluating and judging what is going on. Imagine that you are being a critic of the movie you are watching. How does it make you respond? Ask yourself, "How do I feel about this conversation; how am I judging my own performance?" You are able to notice your emotional response, but as long as you can see yourself "over there" you will not get too caught up in it. You have that particular emotion, but you can also watch it change. Whereas (for most people) first position intensifies the feelings, third position diminishes the feelings because you can distance yourself from the memory.

Another aspect of third position relates to social or peer pressures to conform. You know that you are influenced by what other people say, do, think, and so on. Third position includes understanding the larger systems (family, cultural, institutional, business) that influence you and all of the people in your social groupings. Because "No man is an island ..." you need to think about your relationship to others in terms of moral values, and social norms. Many of your "oughts" and "shoulds" come from thinking about how society will judge your actions. (As these may be unrealistic it would pay you to check them out.) In order to remain a member of a group, to retain their approval, you need to take into consideration the needs of the group or society. You should consider: "If we consider our common goals ..." and find ways of conforming to the agreed norms of that group.

Note: I am putting what is referred to in traditional NLP as the *system position* in third position rather than in fourth, because it has the same function of judging and evaluating. This revised understanding is explained in the work of Peter Young (2004).

Fourth position

Fourth position also has several aspects. In fourth position you think about what is happening from a story point of view and consider likely outcomes: "What happens next?" You use your imagination to foresee probable scenarios and explore the likely consequences of each one. You are also able to see things from a multiple perspective, knowing that everyone has their own story, their own understanding of what is happening, their own way of explaining and making meaning of the situation. A question to ask is, "What is the story? What does this mean to you?"

Fourth position allows the PWS to take an *ironic* view of their situation. That is, they begin to see the funny side of what they are doing in stuttering and blocking. Several PWS have told me that as they came to understand that most blocking and stuttering has its roots in childhood, they laugh at how they were using a behavior that served them in childhood but did the opposite in adulthood. Looked at in this way, the stuttering behavior appears crazy, and the PWS can ask themselves, "Am I bored with doing this? Do I need to go on doing this for the rest of my life?"

Alternatively, the PWS can see their stuttering as part of the story they are telling themselves, and that means they are able to edit or rewrite that story, to give it a better outcome. The story in this case includes the inciting incident (usually in childhood), the stuttering behavior itself, and the way they respond to it. At any point, the PWS can intervene and change things.

Consider how Susan in Chapter One changed the story of her relationship with her parents. When she started the therapy, she was angry, very angry, at her parents, and especially her mother for taking her for "treatment" when there was really nothing wrong with her. She just was having difficulty forming some words. As Susan grew in understanding she changed the story from anger to understanding and forgiveness.

Fifth position

In fifth position you imagine that you are "above all that", having a "God's eye view" of the universe. This fifth position has been described by Marilyn Atkinson (1997) in an unpublished manuscript entitled *Five Central Ideas*, and the idea has been further explored by Peter Young (2004, Chapter 11). This over-arching or spiritual perceptual position offers a universal point of view in which everything is considered. You could see fifth position as having access to all the resources of the universe. Obviously, this provides the widest and most far-reaching perspective of all.

Adopting different points of view

An essential aspect of each perceptual position is its function, its way of working with experience. In fact, you are continually adopting these different points of view. By shifting from one position to another you can step out of an emotionally conflicted situation, you can pay attention to different aspects of your experience. *None of these positions offers a superior position to any other.* Each position has its own function. The wise communicator knows how to move at will from one position to the other. Whatever is happening, you always have sufficient resources for getting some distance on it, and for finding other ways of intervening to change things.

Therefore, when the PWS notices the fear of a block coming on, have them move to each perceptual position in turn to experience how it appears from that point of view. For most PWS, immediately going to fifth position will have the greatest impact in eliminating the fear. However, listen to what the PWS says as they will indicate which position is most beneficial to them. In the process of leading the PWS towards healing, utilize all five positions to provide a variety of perspectives. This assists them in de-stabilizing the locked in nature of their blocking.

A structured approach is useful when you don't know what to do next. It offers a formal way of finding the resources you need to get moving again. It increases your flexibility of mind so that you no longer need to stay stuck in one point of view. Once you stand back, you can evaluate the experience, explore future consequences, and find the resources you need in order to intervene appropriately.

However, the PWS who is stuck finds it extremely difficult to simply step outside the block and go to another position. Therefore, I encourage them to practice this maneuver using the anticipatory anxiety of fearing an upcoming block. Once the PWS can step outside a block at will, they are well on their way to normal fluency.

In using perceptual position thinking for myself, I first associate into the system in first position, and then go to the third position to view objectively my position in relation to others in the team. Then I go second position to each person in the team and then to fourth position to explore the consequences. I switch back and forth through whichever positions I deem appropriate. I love using the fifth position for therapeutic purposes. For people who hold spiritual beliefs, their fifth position is ultimately their spiritual place. Because I am a Christian, when I go to fifth position, I view myself as being with Jesus. I am way "up there" with Him looking down on myself way down here.

If you hold spiritual beliefs, think of some event in the past that you still have negative emotions about when you recall it. Now imagine yourself leaving your body and going up and being with God, or Spirit, or whatever you call this concept. Once you are up there viewing things from your fifth position, seeing yourself down here, how does that affect the negative emotions around that experience? Going "up there" is most relaxing and calming to many people, and far better than Prozac! Most PWS when they get into their fifth position become much more fluent – and many become totally fluent. The clinician's job is to teach them how to access that state at will.

In the following exercise you will be leading the PWS to move among the five different positions. I suggest you begin by having them to recall a major time they blocked. Direct them to go through the following steps asking them the questions in quotation marks:

Exercise 3.8: Changing perceptual positions

1. First position – Recall the last time you blocked. Notice how you feel inside the block.
2. Second position – Float out of your body and into the other person's body. Experience that blocking from the other person's perspective.
3. Third position – Dissociate or "pop out" of your body and observe the situation from this objective viewpoint.
4. Fourth position – Imagine watching these two people in front of you from the point of view of the story that is unfolding.
5. Fifth position – Float up out of your body to your highest level of thinking. From this position become compassionately aware of that "you" down there all full of fear and anxiety.

1. **First position** – "Recall the last major time you blocked when in the presence of another person."

   "Associate into your body (first position) by seeing what you saw, hearing what you heard, and feeling what you felt."

   "Do you still feel the same negative emotions you felt then?" (They probably will.)

2. **Second position** – "Now imagine yourself floating out of your body and floating into the body of the person you were talking with. Stand (or sit) as they are standing (or sitting). Looking through their eyes at that person who looks like you, notice how you appear while blocking. What are the key things that you are aware of? Staying in role, as this other person, notice how you feel about that person in front of you who is blocking."

   A major part of the problem of blocking is that the person places too much emphasis upon what other people *might* be thinking. However that is more of a mixed second and third position judgment, rather than a true second position experience. It is important to gather information by adopting the other person's *actual* perspective rather than projecting your own story onto the other person and *assuming* what you think they are experiencing.

3. **Third position** – "Now, dissociate yourself from that event. Mentally step back so that you can see both yourself and the other person during the blocking episode. How do you respond

to that you who is doing the blocking? What judgments are you making about that situation? And as a result of making those judgments, what emotions are activated."

"As you look at both yourself and the other person, did you really have a justifiable reason to be all tense and fearful?"

"Was your tension justifiable? Was the person really a threat to you? Or, did you just *imagine* that the person was a threat?"

4. **Fourth position** – "Now imagine that you are watching a story unfolding in front of you. You know who the characters are – but why are they behaving like that? Is that the story you want to be watching? How would it be if you were to tell the story another way? Could you make it into a comedy, rather than a tragedy? There is a saying, 'One day you'll look back on this and laugh … So why wait?' You could laugh now at that crazy behavior! OK, if it's serious, then maybe you could rewrite the drama so that it has a happy ending. You may have to do some serious editing, but you can make the story be whatever you want it to be. After all, you created that story in the first place. And hey, what are those other characters in the movie up to? Could they do better? You bet they could. So give them some acting training, give them some new skills, some new objectives – ones that lead to a better outcome. Remember: it's a story! Each person is following their own script. So how about editing those scripts so you have a movie you would rather see?"

5. **Fifth position** – "Now float up above all that, rise up into a fifth position, way out in the universe. If you have a belief in God, then be there with God and all creation."

Note: I suggest that you find out ahead of time about their spiritual beliefs before mentioning going to God to them. They may have another name for this. You need to respect their beliefs. If they do have a belief in God this will be their ultimate fifth position and a very powerful resource state for them, so use it! Also use their metaphor for where they are moving to. Are they rising *up*, or moving *back*, or going *beyond* …?

"Viewing the experience of blocking from this position, how does the situation change from that position? How do you feel? Do you feel more relaxed and calm being *universal, above all that,* or *way out there?"*

"If you believe in God, or some Universal Being, how do you feel being in the presence of God? What happens to the tension, fear, anxiety, that you were experiencing in your body – in your chest, neck, throat or jaw – now that you are in the presence of deity?"

"Had you gone to this position during that block, what would have happened?"

Applying your fifth position to fear and anxiety

"To complete this process be totally and completely in fifth position. Allow this feeling to permeate the whole of your being. And then allow this even more ... Allow your universe to be filled with love, acceptance, appreciation and awe. And now simply allow all of this, all the resources that are available to you in this state, to flow down into that you who was experiencing the fear and the anxiety of blocking and stuttering. And notice what happens to that you in first position as they receive these resources ... What happens to those fears and anxieties when your fifth position meets your first position?"

Note: Many who have overcome blocking have found the fifth position extremely helpful. They learn how to go there at will through consistent practice. In the fifth position most people are very relaxed and calm which provides the proper state for fluency. If you find this difficult to do in your mind's eye, you may find that marking out each position on the floor and then physically visiting each position in turn and sensing what each position feels like will enable you to have this experience.

We have now covered the basic skills and essential thinking needed for making changes. However, there are many refinements, many details about how you can do this elegantly, with precision, and we will explore these in the next three chapters.

Chapter Four

Stories about Stuttering

Models of the world

For sure, the PWS never leaves home without their beliefs relating to blocking and stuttering. These beliefs help construct and define their evolving model of the world which they use to navigate through life and to understand what they experience. If they tell themselves that they are a person of worth, they will live their life one way. If, on the other hand, they view themselves in a negative light with little or no power to navigate their world, they live their life in a more restricted way. A person's model of the world deter mines how they experience life at any moment. The good news is that it is possible to change their model of the world, as Linda Rounds did in her story (Appendix B).

We make meaning of our experience through stories which tell us "how things happen". We have stories for the big things: the story of my life, and for the small things, how to make a cup of coffee. When a PWS anticipates an upcoming conversation, then tell themselves a story that creates the fear in them that they will block. This story is based on past experiences in which they "always" blocked in certain contexts. (The times when they didn't block got erased from the memory. Only those memories which support their limiting belief that "they have always blocked and they always will" are registered!)

The stories we tell about the events of our lives are important because they have the power to transform and heal or to trauma- tize and destroy. We use various scripts, plots, and themes to frame things. The narrative structure organizes and maintains a sophisti- cated belief system which can keep us in distress and limit our choices, or create an empowering and resourceful way of living. How would you describe the story of your life in one word? Would it be: Failure, Victim, Oppressor, Fugitive, Loser ... or Hero, Leader, Healer, Explorer, Mentor, Guide ... ?

As I mentioned in Chapter Two, using one word or a short phrase to encapsulate the meaning of a whole life-time's experience is both an interesting challenge, and a gross distortion of reality. Therefore treat the result of this exercise as simply a "snapshot" which belongs to the moment in which it was created, rather than being an eternal truth.

So we need to know how the PWS makes meaning of their world, in terms of the stories or movies they run which tell them: "what happens next?"

In the last chapter you did a thought experiment about sucking a lemon, and your body responded with increased salivation. In other words, stories are "real" in the sense that they have consequences. (If you just noticed your salivation increasing, that's the power of a trigger!) However, whether something is real or not is not the point. What matters is that the story you are telling yourself has consequences. Because if the story does not give you what you want, you can change it. Simple. You already know this from your personal experience, because you are constantly updating the stories that make your life liveable. For example, you have picked up stories about using mobile phones, about responding to terrorist attacks, and so on. However, the PWS has a stuttering story which has been told so often that it has acquired the qualities of permanence. And what are those qualities? Well, we will examine them in a moment.

Anticipatory anxiety

Your states affect everything you do. At any one time, your state governs how you perceive and interpret your environment, how you communicate, how you behave, and in addition, how well you remember what you have learned in the past. You know that when you are tired, or have been consuming mind-altering substances such as caffeine, alcohol, or other drugs of choice, your ability to recall your past alters. And when you are anxious about what may happen, that narrows your focus of what you pay attention to.

When the PWS considers an upcoming conversation in which they expect to block, they usually imagine a movie of themselves blocking during that conversation. Their body *fulfils* the movie's expectations and this creates a state of fear which then gives rise to actual blocking (Figure 4.1). This anticipatory anxiety drives a lot of blocking and stuttering.

If you are a PWS check this out for yourself. Think about an upcoming conversation with someone with whom you usually block. Notice what you do. In all probability, you imagine a picture or a movie of seeing yourself blocking with that person. The mind-body system does not really distinguish between "real" and "imaginary" movies. You know that if you watch a scary Hollywood movie, your mind-body pumps out the adrenalin to get you ready to run! So when you run your own movie of an impending conversation, your state shifts in readiness for what you *expect* to happen. You block because it's a story about blocking. Your body obliges; you feel muscles tensing up.

If you are not a PWS, create an imaginary movie of some future event that will create anxiety or even fear for you. For example, being found out and called into the boss's office. (Did something like that ever happen at school?) Notice how your state changes as you create that imaginary movie. And now think of something really pleasant, such as completing an important task (sending off your tax return!) and relaxing ... You can always choose to feel good, whenever you like!

In order to change a PWS's stuttering behavior, to interrupt their blocking strategy, you have to get inside their inner world and determine which stories, thoughts or beliefs are responsible for the blocking. I will suggest some techniques for exposing those stories and the images and language patterns that support them. Then, by contrast, you need to discover the frames of meaning which allow them to speak fluently, and teach the PWS to change their blocking story to a fluency story. Remember that the PWS already knows how to speak fluently in some contexts. That means they already have those frames available.

Movies in the mind

There are two key components that affect your state: the movie you imagine of what is going to happen; and the language you use to talk to yourself about it. First let's look closely at the movies people make in the mind, because changing the *qualities* of those movies changes their meaning. For example, take that anxiety movie you were just imagining, and create a pleasantly relaxing mood simply by adjusting its appearance. Turn down the brightness, have muted colors, slow the action, play some soft music in the background … and notice your state now.

Think of how a Hollywood movie establishes a mood. Romantic comedies are usually sunny, lots of bright colors. Having a static camera in beautiful scenery, with soothing orchestral music, is calming; it reassures you that pleasant things will happen. On the other hand, a movie made in black and white, using a hand-held camera, and which involves rushing about in the dark with a thumping heartbeat soundtrack is an effective way of increasing uncertainty and tension. Horror movies are often full of shadows, half-seen events, extreme close-ups … just add some screeching violins …!

People who block and stutter are skilled in creating horror movies in their minds. Who needs the "Master of Horror" Stephen King when they can do their own movie making? Sometimes they scare the hell out of themselves about an upcoming conversation by making it look like a horror movie. They distort the image of the other person who then judges them because they block, or laughs at them, dismisses them as worthless, and so on.

It is easy to create a scary public-speaking movie. Just imagine the vast hall, the huge audience … staring at you … waiting for you … to start … stuttering. That can generate enough fear and anxiety to make anyone stutter! With intense fear, the general arousal syndrome kicks in, the adrenalin starts flowing, ready for fight or flight (Figure 4.1). This response keeps you alive when under real threat, but it does not serve you when you live in that state all the time. Since speaking is a large part of living, then living in constant fear and anxiety of speaking and keeping your general arousal syndrome constantly activated is not good.

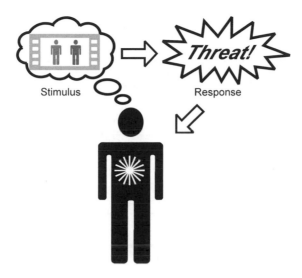

Figure 4.1: Fight or flight?

CASE STUDY 9

I emailed this question to a client, Robert, who had a problem of blocking when he was delivering a public speech: "What is there about public speaking that triggers tension and fear of speaking?" Robert replied:

> The fact that there are all those people staring at me and expecting me to deliver a perfectly fluent speech in a short amount of time. All of the pressure, tension, and fear comes from those expectations. The more I try to speak like a non-stutterer, the tighter my throat gets. I think that if every person in this world stuttered and stuttering was the norm, I might actually enjoy public speaking.

Later in my email I asked Robert, "If you absolutely did not care what other people thought, what would happen to your speech?" He replied:

> I would think that my speech would improve greatly. It is really hard to say for sure how my speech would be in that situation because we don't live in a society where people do not care or notice if someone stutters. However, I am positive that there would be no nervousness or anxiety before a speaking situation.

I directed him to "compare and contrast your state of mind between when you are alone and when you stutter. What are the differences? What are you seeing, hearing, feeling? How are you talking to yourself differently between fluency and stuttering?" He responded:

When I am alone, I couldn't care less if I stutter or not. Consequently, there is no anxiety, nervousness, or tightness in my chest/throat. There is no need to anticipate or mentally prepare for a speaking situation *where I have a chance to humiliate myself*. Therefore, every sound comes out perfectly. When I stutter, I always find myself rehearsing in my mind the exact words I am going to say because I may need to substitute some trouble words. There is always an anxiety and fear of what will happen when I stutter or block. *How will the audience react? Will they laugh or look uncomfortable watching me strain to get the words out? Will I be a failure in their eyes?* [italics added]

This probably sounds familiar to a PWS. Note Robert's very first statement: "The fact that there are all those people ... expecting me to deliver a perfectly fluent speech ... All of the pressure/tension fear comes from those expectations." This statement goes right to one of the central problems of blocking – fear of what others may think about one's speech.

Robert's stated belief is also unrealistic. What audiences really want is for the speaker to be entertaining, interesting, lively. They want to have a good time, and they want the speaker to have a good time too. They are very forgiving, just as long as the presenter is engaging directly with them, being authentic, speaking from the heart. It is very common for "nervous" presenters to imagine the worst, when they would be better off remembering that audiences are generally supportive.

Note that Robert said that his expectations of a fluent speech are a "fact." That doesn't leave any room for exceptions. How does he know this? Does he go and ask each one individually? No. He is mind-reading the audience.

I have italicized some key statements in his last paragraph. Notice Robert's fear of humiliating himself; of being laughed at; his fear of them being uncomfortable if he can't get the words out. These are all very common fears about what others *might* think of the PWS's speech. So what kind of movie for generating blocking does the PWS make as they anticipate the next encounter? Probably of the scary variety with a voice-over soundtrack to match.

One client has a tremendous fear of talking to people on the phone. Of major concern are those people with whom he does business. Before he calls them, the first thing he does is to create a picture in his head of the other person answering the phone. Immediately, after he sees the picture, he starts talking to himself about his fear of losing this client.

The things you say to yourself

Movies also have dialog. Your movies probably do, because most people talk to themselves on the inside. Occasionally it's out loud, but more often their internal dialog – mind-talk – is chattering away much of the time. Although you may think this is insignificant, what you say matters because it affects your behavior.

Providing a running commentary on how they will fail does the PWS no favors. If the PWS is talking to themselves about fearing they will block (anticipatory anxiety), it's highly likely they will have themselves a horror movie, and that certainly won't improve things. The good news is that if they can talk themselves into a down state, they can also talk themselves up by changing the dialogue so that the old pattern becomes redundant. They need to change the way they talk to themselves, the kind of language they use, and the way it sounds (the tonality), as that will radically alter the power and the meaning of the movie.

Notice *what* you are saying to yourself:

Are you talking about what you want, and the good things in life, or are you putting yourself (and others) down, forever complaining about what has happened, and blaming others for causing it? One idea leads to another, and you're back layering negative stuff onto that original event. The feelings continue to create webs of negative thoughts that are difficult to escape from.

And *how* you are saying it:

> It really does matter how PWS talk to themselves on the inside. What tone of voice do you habitually use? If you have never stopped to notice how you sound inside your mind, then take a moment to listen. And then think about your response to that kind of voice. You know how you respond when someone else's voice is boring, scratchy, whining, argumentative, or playing "poor me." Instead of a moaning, depressing or angry voice, choose one that is pleasant, confident, reassuring … By using empowering language they can intensify their state. For example, by thinking, "I can speak fluently. I do it whenever I choose" – and meaning it – it will become a reality for them.

Here is how you can turn around a dialog of what could have been a self-destructive internal:

> I have to make that phone call to order that book. I blocked the last time I called that salesman. He reminds me of my dad. I was afraid of my dad. But wait a minute. He isn't my dad, and I am no longer a child. I am a grown adult. I don't have to worry about my dad calling me stupid. Goodness, dad isn't standing over me, watching everything I do. And I do know how to speak fluently, without holding back. I'm fluent when I talk to my friends. I know what I will do: if I start to get anxious when I'm talking to him, I will pretend that he's an old friend and we're just having a chat. Hey, I think that will work!

What you say to yourself, and the way you say it, really does make a difference in how you feel, and that affects what you do, and how you come across to others.

Changing the *kind* of movie in your mind sends signals to your body which create a state of well-being. This already happens with some of the people you communicate with. You don't bother to run your blocking movie with those people, and just get on with the conversation. You don't even think about how you are speaking or coming across; you just carry on talking comfortably. This is fluency.

Editing the movies in your mind

Note: Before working with other people using these techniques, it is important that you have experienced using them for yourself. Practice these interventions so that you can do them easily, know what to expect, and what works for you. Remember that other people may do things differently ….

How exactly does a PWS create a blocking movie? Before a potentially anxiety-producing event, the PWS imagines a movie with any or all of the following: pictures, sounds, feelings, smells, tastes, and commentary. In terms of the way people process different kinds of information, pictures (Visual) are by far the most important. Sounds (Auditory) come next, and feelings (Kinesthetic) after that. Now by feelings, the reference is not to emotions (more about emotions later), but to their ability to feel temperature, pressure, texture, humidity, and so on. This is about both external (tactile) and internal (proprioceptive) feelings. Taste and Smell are important for a minority, but these qualities are often missing from most people's mental movies.

People who do not visualize well use their other senses more. If a PWS is not aware of creating a movie with pictures, ask them about the sound-track. Are they talking to themselves, providing a voice-over description of what is happening? If so, what kind of voice do they use? What kind of tonality? Where does that voice seem to come from? These are the type of questions worth asking the PWS to discover just how they structure their movies.

Movie qualities

Every movie has qualities in terms of how it appears, how it is constructed, rather than the content, what it is about. For example, in terms of the qualities of the images, notice whether the picture is big, bright, panoramic, in saturated color; or dim and distant, with a border, with muted or dark colors. These *structural* qualities may have major implications for blocking.

There are many distinctions that we can make in terms of the qualities of the pictures, sounds, feelings and so on. Figure 4.2 lists

Visual (pictures)	Auditory (sounds)	Kinesthetic (feelings)
Brightness	Pitch	Pressure
Contrast	Timbre	Location
Color and saturation	Tempo	Extent
Density and transparency	Volume	Shape
Size	Rhythm	Texture
Clarity and focus	Duration	Temperature
Depth	Distance	Humidity
Distance and location	Location	Movement
Moving, still or looping	Clarity	Duration
Edge or border	Continuous or interrupted	Intensity
Associated/dissociated	Movement	Frequency

Figure 4.2: Sensory qualities

some of the key qualities in the visual, auditory and kinesthetic systems.

Any movie can be analyzed in terms of its qualities; the structure, the attributes of the pictures, sounds and feelings. Each quality, on its own or in combination with others, provides meaning, and people are skilled at interpreting such combinations, to know whether they are "good" or "bad", "safe" or "dangerous", "interesting" or "boring" and so on. It is also the case that as the qualities vary, from light to dark, from loud to soft ..., so does the meaning. Let's play with this for a moment.

> Think of a pleasant experience, and see it as a movie. Notice how far that movie of that pleasant experience is from you. Is it close or distant? Is the movie in bright colors, desaturated or pastel colors, or in black and white? Is it a broad panoramic picture or small like a snapshot? Is it full, realistic detail, or more like a cartoon or line drawing? There are many such variations in how people create their internal movies. However, there are general patterns. For example, most people make their pleasant movies rich in detail, up close, in color and usually panoramic (but there are always exceptions so you have to find out). Although most people have never been asked such questions before, all they have to do is to look and tell you the answers.
>
> If the PWS is unable to create a visual movie, ask them how they primarily experience the pleasant memory: as a feeling or as a sound? If not visually, most will do it with feelings. If so, ask them

the qualities of the feelings: "Where do you feel it? Is the feeling heavy or light or somewhere in between? Does it have a temperature? Describe to me how you experience that feeling." Use the sensory-based quality descriptions as in Figure 4.2 rather than anything abstract.

Play with your movie of the pleasant experience just to experience how changing its properties affects its meaning. If it is close to you, move it away and notice if it changes the strength of the pleasant feeling. If it is in color, make it black & white. Turn it into a cartoon. How do these adjustments affect the feeling of the experience? Changing the structure of your movies is one way of changing their meaning, and the responses you have to the them.

Certain combinations of qualities, such as *close, colored, bright, no border*, and so on, provide a way of encoding and differentiating concepts such as *real − unreal, past − future, important − trivial*, and so on. We also use these symbolic codes for identifying emotions such as "fear" and "courage" and for distinguishing between different states, such as "procrastinating" or "going for it". Knowing how the person structures a particular experience means that they can deliberately change the meaning of that experience by manipulating its qualities so that it resembles something more desirable.

These attributes also turn up in the metaphors we use. Consider the following statements:

> "This way of thinking has a bright future."
> "That's music to my ears."
> "He came down heavy like a ton of bricks."
> "Something smells fishy about her proposal."
> "That leaves a nasty taste in the mouth."

These metaphorical sayings often give us a glimpse of the way the speaker's has constructed the pictures, sounds, feelings, and so on, into a coherent story. Although some of these metaphorical sayings are clichés, they often provide a literal description of the person's model of the world.

Exercise 4.1: Qualities of the movie

This exercise helps the PWS become aware of the particular way they imagine their story or movie. People tend to take this for granted, and assume that everyone does this in the same way. They do not. What people do in their minds is idiosyncratic.

You are going to ask the PWS to imagine two different experiences of speaking to another person: in one they imagine themselves blocking, in the other they are speaking fluently. If they need help in bringing the picture to conscious awareness, you could, for example, ask them to describe the other person, male or female, what they are wearing, and so on. Then they are going to compare these two images to find the significant differences. Refer to Figure 4.2 for a list of the visual, auditory and kinesthetic qualities.

Overview

1. Associate into a time when you were fluent noting your visual, auditory and kinesthetic experience.
2. Associate into a time of blocking and note your visual, auditory and kinesthetic experience of this experience.
3. Make a note of the visual, auditory and kinesthetic qualities of both experiences and compare and contrast them.
4. Practice changing the qualities of the blocking image to resemble the fluency image.
5. Play with editing your own movies.

1. Recall a recent time when you were very fluent. Imagine yourself back there in that state of fluency. Be looking out of your eyes, seeing what is around you, including the other people. Hear all the sounds around you and be aware of how it feels being totally fluent now. If you are talking to yourself, notice the qualities of your voice.

    "See what you saw then. Hear the sounds you heard at that time and feel the feelings you felt."

2. When they can do this for states of fluency, have them do the same thing for blocking. If they have a strong emotional reaction, tell them not to get too bound up with it, and remind them that this is in their imagination, and that they can change out of this state whenever they want to.

"See what you saw then. Hear the sounds you heard at that time and feel the feelings you felt."

3. Compare and contrast these two experiences. Make a note of the *visual* qualities. Write these down side-by-side on a piece of paper. Use Figure 4.2 as a guide. After listing the visual qualities, list the key *auditory* and the key *kinesthetic* qualities. There should be some differences between the two lists. Which appear to be the key differences? Which qualities tell you that one movie is about fluency, and the other about blocking?

4. Practice changing the qualities of the blocking image so that it resembles the fluency image. Now choose one of the main differences in visual, and lead the PWS to change that visual quality of the Blocking image to be like the visual quality of the Fluency picture. For example, if the location and distance is markedly different, direct the PWS to move the picture of the blocking experience into the same location as the fluent experience. Then you can either have them move things back to how they were, or they can add further adjustments to any of the other key qualities of the Blocking experience into the same qualities of the Fluency experience.

5. Have them play with "editing" their movie as they experiment with the qualities to develop a more suitable experience for the formerly blocking experience.

Exercise 4.2: Type of movie

Another way of finding out the type of difference between the two kinds of movies is to ask your PWS client about the general qualities of their movies.

Just take a moment to relax as though you are in a cinema, and you are going to watch a movie of a time when you were blocking. As you observe the movie, notice:

1. What *kind* of movie is it (in terms of genre, or what it looks like)? Is this movie typical of the movies you run in your mind when you block?

2. Now run a movie of a similar kind of interaction but where you don't block. What kind of movie is that, in terms of qualities, or genre, theme, and so on?

3. What happens in the movies of you blocking or stuttering? How does it start? What happens next? How does it finish?

4. How do you feel as you watch yourself in that Blocking movie? Embarrassed? Angry? Hesitant?

5. What happens in the movies when you are fluent, and don't block and stutter? How does it start? What happens next? How does it finish? How do you feel?

6. Compare these two movies, and notice in how many ways they differ.

The story or strategy for blocking can also be edited, changed, or directed to give a different outcome. This is why you need to know the movie's original structure, because then you can adjust or modify any of the attributes to find out which qualities when changed alter the emotional effect of that movie.

Associating/dissociating

Remember the difference between being dissociated and being associated: do you see yourself in the movie or not? (See Chapter Three.) It is an important feature of editing movies in the mind. There is a relationship between the movie and the person imagining it. Does the PWS see themselves in that image, or is the image what they would see as though looking from their own eyes? If they do see themselves, do they notice that they are actually blocking? In my experience, when the PWS imagines themselves blocking, they probably do not see themselves in the imaginary picture. They imagine themselves talking to the other person and all they see is the other person. They are experiencing those fears and anxieties just as if it were real.

For most people, but not all, imagining themselves associated inside a picture intensifies the emotion. If the PWS runs a movie in their mind of a forthcoming conversation and they imagine themselves *inside* that movie blocking when they speak to the other person, then, in all likelihood, their mind-body system will say, "OK, I will do that. When you are in front of that person talking, I will make sure that you block/stutter."

The PWS is more likely to speak fluently when they see themselves (dissociated) engaging with that other person. Ask the PWS to mentally step back, to dissociate, so that they are watching the movie as if it were on a screen in the cinema. They are likely to be very critical of what they see themselves doing. While they are thinking in that way, I ask them, "What have you learned from this? What would you like to change?" There is always something to be learned from every experience, and that starts when the person is judging or evaluating their performance. Then they can begin to coach themselves to do better.

And then for practice, after they see themselves speaking fluently with the other person, they may wish to imagine themselves there in front of the person (associated) and imagine how it would be if they were speaking fluently.

Changing the meaning of the context

Once during a first session with a woman who blocks, she told me that she could not force herself to block when she was by herself. I inquired about the difference between her state when she was alone and her state of blocking. She said, "When I am by myself I have confidence because *no one can hurt me.*" The major factor in creating state of blocking was avoiding being hurt by someone else. Obviously, when she was alone that fear was not triggered. But in company she became concerned with the fear of being hurt. She was focusing on the fear inside her instead of concentrating on the purpose of the communication. Blocking, like most of our problems, is an inside job.

Therefore one way out of the difficulty is to change the meaning of the context which triggers the blocking response.

Changing the trigger

There are three main areas for making changes:

1. On a behavioral or body level, change the stimulus-response connection. By altering the meaning of the external trigger it loses its power, and fails to produce the blocking response. As the clinician you want the PWS to link a more powerful trigger (sight, sound, sensation, movement, gesture, word) to a state or strategy that will lead them to fluency. Instead of an authority-figure creating fear and blocking they trigger a resource state or strategy for speaking fluently (see The Swish Pattern in Chapter Six).

2. On a cognitive or mind level, change the person's beliefs about themselves, so that the blocking becomes "irrelevant." This is a consequence of the Meta-stating process (see Chapter Three): the PWS applies a more powerful resource state which enfeebles the old pattern. The PWS stops concentrating on themselves: they stop running their old disaster movies, stop imagining those dreadful judgments of others, and start thinking more about the other person. They get on with the conversation, knowing they have something important or vital to say and pay attention to the other person as they communicate with them, calmly, confidently, and successfully.

3. On a spiritual level, probably the single most effective way of changing the trigger to a resource state is for the PWS to immediately go to their fifth position (see Chapter Three). This is especially true if the person has some really powerful spiritual and religious beliefs and values in that position. Indeed, as I have mentioned, once the PWS can go to that position/ state at will, they are well on their way to normal fluency.

In practice, you will be working with all of these ways. But first it is useful to untangle some of the complexity. For example: discover the nature of the triggers. Are they primarily visual (a particular location, or how someone looks) or auditory (the sound of someone's voice, or a particular word). To change their response the meaning they give to those triggers has to change. When the PWS thinks about speaking with their boss, they run the movie:

"I have to go into that office and speak with my boss. He always scares me. I know I will block in front of him. I always do." So it seems that both the sight of the office and the appearance of the boss can be triggers for the state. Therefore it is necessary to set up beforehand some other meaning for those cues. For example, "The office is just an office. It just happens to be where my boss is at the moment, but other people have also been based there, and will be in the future." For the boss, the PWS can realise that "My boss is just another human being, with worries and cares, who wants to do the best for the organization, but who is also insecure in some areas of their life. Maybe I need to be in a position of strength where I can be supportive to them." To hold these beliefs, the PWS needs to accept the thought, "I am a competent worker who goes beyond what is expected. I recognize my own strengths and weaknesses, and I learn from them. And I can be a role model for others." Changing the meanings of your environment means that you will act differently.

Strategy/pattern interrupts

Although a blocking strategy usually runs automatically, out of conscious awareness, it is possible to stop it before it gets going. This must be true or you would never change any behavior. Your goal is to teach the PWS how to interrupt their blocking strategy so that they can do something more useful. An *interrupt* is anything that stops a strategy from running. The logical place to make a change is where it begins: to alter the meaning of the inciting incident – the stimulus or trigger – that sets the strategy going. Your task then is to help the PWS find how their strategy can be frustrated, prevented or sabotaged.

An interrupt has to be powerful enough to jump the person right out of the groove. The interrupt can be a physical gesture, a sound, a movement, or a code word. For example, the person could just say "Stop!" Initially the interrupt may work better if it comes from someone else, which means the PWS should give permission to a trusted other person to interrupt them every time they start blocking. Later the PWS must initiate their own interrupts.

Remember that people are already skilled in doing this. You know that you can inhibit your behavior when conditions change. You can probably remember a time when you were engaged in a slanging match, and then something happened and you thought "This is ridiculous! Why am I doing this?" and you changed your state, began to laugh, and the whole tense situation altered and everyone relaxed. This would be an example of shifting your point of view to fourth position and seeing the funny side of things. The interruption changes your state and that affects your behaviour. By not allowing the blocking strategy to run, the PWS is open to find better ways of communicating to other people.

When they interrupt the pattern, the PWS must stop what they are doing and pause long enough to access an appropriate resource state which they have chosen beforehand. It could be a resource such as *courage, faith, determination* or *calmness* – it does not matter what it is, only that it leads the PWS away from the old groove, and towards fluency. One client remarked upon first learning about state interrupts:

> I used to scream really loud inside my head to interrupt my state. I got the idea when I was reading Tony Robbins' book, *Awaken the Giant Within*. It worked pretty well. If I was alone in the house I would scream out loud, really loud. It made me laugh every time because it was so ridiculous. It served its purpose … my state was interrupted every time.

Erasing fearful movies of painful memories

This process (adapted from the NLP Fast Phobia Cure) can dramatically assist the PWS to change their response to the fear behind the blocking. It is designed to scramble the visual images of the movie that creates the fear.

A phobia is an automatic response to a specific triggering situation: a spider, a lift, a snake, and so on. Blocking is similar to a phobic response in that something in the context triggers the behavior. With a phobia it is usually easier to see what sets it off, but with blocking the trigger is often a more subtle aspect of the context –

the associated meaning and expectations. However, whatever the trigger, the phobic response or the blocking and stuttering occurs, and therefore the technique can be used successfully in these cases. This process takes the juice out of those painful memories – those childhood experiences of embarrassment or shame – which led to the blocking and stuttering.

Dealing with old unpleasant memories

When you think about unpleasant events that happened long ago, your mind often seems to compulsively say, "Play it again!" And so you get to watch a full-color, three-dimensional movie of that old memory and the opportunity to feel really bad again!

How do you stop this happening? One way is to scramble the movie so that it loses its coherence and thus its power over you and your emotions. Although you could edit the qualities of a movie one at a time, it is also possible to quickly revise the whole movie at once.

Exercise 4.3: The fast rewind process

Overview

1. Step back from your painful memory.
2. Step back from the you watching the movie.
3. Let the old movie play out as you watch from a protected place.
4. Step into the movie and fast rewind.
5. Repeat the process several times.
6. Test.

Note: You could run this pattern effectively on any horror movie that limits you in some way. Often times the fear is not based in reality but on the consequences you imagine from a composite story based on several historical events. If that story limits you, then use this process for eliminating those painful memories.

Lead the PWS through the following steps:

1. **Step back from your painful memory.**
   - Begin with a negative thought that sets off painful emotional reactions. Pick an childhood memory of a blocking incident that "rattles your cage", that elicits strong emotional feelings. The memory could be about an occasion when other people made fun of you, or shamed you because of your blocking.

   - Now imagine yourself sitting in a movie theater looking at the movie screen. On that screen put a still, black-and-white snapshot of the younger you just prior to that fearful, hurtful, or traumatic episode.

   - Good. This represents the scene immediately prior to the fearful memory. Now sit back and look at the snapshot of the younger you. Do so with the awareness that you have taken a spectator's position and can observe that younger you.

   - This enables you to gain "psychological distance" from the old pain. From this spectator position you can *begin to learn* from that old memory: "As you now see that event from a safe distance and can look from it through the eyes of an objective adult, what do you learn from that experience?"

In working with PWS, I find many who have gone through terrible emotional, physical or sexual abuse as children. Their emotional response to these events has become expressed in the muscles for breathing and speaking and has led to their blocking and stuttering. Following such experiences, the child often grows up hanging onto the pain, anger and fear as a reminder to not to put themselves in any position where they may be abused again. This is how blocking and stuttering become a protective device. Therefore in this step the person can learn that they are no longer a child and that they have adult resources to now handle such threatening moments. They learn that not everyone in this world is out to abuse them; they do not have to be "on guard" all the time – a very common state for PWS.

2. **Step back from the you watching the movie.**
   - Now imagine floating out of your body as you watch that snapshot on the screen. You are floating all the way up to the back of the theater and up into the projection booth.

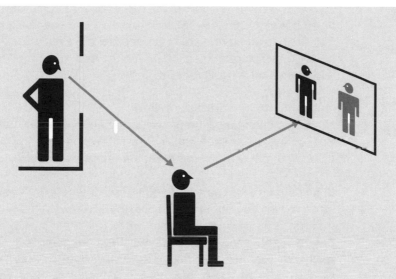

Figure 4.3: The fast rewind process

Place an imaginary piece of Plexiglas in the viewing window in front of you for greater protection. From this new point of view, see yourself down there in the auditorium, the back of your head, as *that you* is sitting there watching the snapshot of the *younger you* on the screen (Figure 4.3).

- If at any time you begin to feel uncomfortable, then just put your hands on the Plexiglas in front of you and remind your self to feel safe and secure in the control booth.

- Feel the calmness of this sense of distance.

3. **Let the old memory play out as you watch it from the pro-tected place.**
   - Still in the projection booth, observe yourself watching the younger you on the movie screen as you let the initial snap-shot turn into a black-and-white movie. Watch that movie of the incident until it plays out to the end.

   - Now watch the whole movie again. Let it play out beyond the end to a time when that *younger you* felt safe and okay again. You have moved beyond that traumatic event to scene of safety, security and comfort.

- If you have to jump forward several years to a scene of comfort, do that. Jump forward to an appropriate event, and then freeze that picture and splice it onto the end of the movie so that it ends on a positive note.

4. **Step into the movie and fast rewind.**
    - Now, step into that scene of comfort at the end of the movie. Step in and experience it fully. See everything around you in color. You may want some pleasant music playing.

    - In just a moment, you are going to do something surprising, so let me tell you about it. You are going to rewind the movie from this scene of comfort backwards to the initial snapshot before the beginning of the episode. You are going to do this really fast. So fast that happens in a fraction of a second. Now you have seen movies or videos run backwards haven't you? Good. Well this one is going to rewind at a high speed, but with this difference: you are going to be *inside* it.

    From that (associated) point of view, you will see all the people performing their actions backwards. They walk and talk backwards. You walk and talk in reverse. Everything happens in a fusion of sights and a jumbling of sounds as the movie whizzes back to the beginning.

    - Ready? Okay, associate into the comfort scene at the end of the movie, see what you see, hear what you hear, feel all of those feelings of comfort, OK-ness, joy, relaxation, whatever is there. Do so fully and completely.

    - Now rewind: *Whooooosh*! Go all the way back to the beginning. As fast as that. Even faster than that …

    - Good. Clear the screen of your mind. How did that feel … rewinding from inside the movie? Weird, huh?

5. **Repeat the process five times.**
    - Having arrived back to the *snapshot* at the beginning, clear the screen in your mind. Open your eyes and look around. Breathe!

- Let's do this again. Begin at the *scene of comfort* at the end again, and *as soon as* you step it, feel, see, and hear it fully ... rewind the movie ... do it even faster this time.

- Good. Repeat four more times. Of course, as you do this over and over your mind will become more and more proficient and the rewind will go faster and faster until the rewind takes only a fraction of a second each time. *Whoooooosh*!!

6. **Test.**
   - Okay. Stop, and break state. Stand up, walk around ...

   - Now, try to recall that original memory of the trauma and try really hard to see if you can get those feelings back. Try as hard as you can to step into the scene and feel the full weight of the emotions.

Note: The emotional impact of that incident should have diminished or disappeared. Check that this is so. This pattern is about 70 to 80% effective. Like all NLP and Neuro-Semantic Patterns, nothing works all the time for all people. As a next step, use the Drop Down Through technique in Chapter Six.

Rewriting your story

Sometimes a PWS will say, "If I could only go back and start again ... then I would not start blocking or stuttering." "I want to go back and re-live my life so that I would not have to put up with what my parents did, and I could avoid having a speech pathologist saying there was something wrong with me."

Your stories help you make sense of how you are *right now*. They are not about the "truth" of what "really" happened, but your current understanding of your model of the world. And because this is a story, it can be changed, edited, rewritten, or even abandoned.

The story that the PWS is telling you usually begins some time in their childhood. There may be a specific inciting event that makes sense in terms of the story: "It was when X happened that this feeling of being inadequate really struck home ..."

One way of rewriting the story is to go back to that inciting incident – whatever *starts* the story – and change the conditions surrounding it so that *it doesn't happen in that way*. This is not about actually changing "the past" – what happened, happened. It is about changing the PWS's current *interpretation* of what happened. After all, they were a child at the time, and without the understanding, the coping mechanisms, the strategies for change that they now have as an adult. Treating the story as a fiction makes changing someone's emotional response to "their past" much easier. You could, for example, imagine going back to the inciting incident and giving those significant others the resources *they* needed at the time. In your imagination, you are unlimited.

The following process provides a means of rewriting the story so that the PWS can go back and change the story of their life. I have revised Michael Hall's original version (Hall, 2001–2002) to make it more appropriate for use with PWS. Several PWS have found the following pattern helpful. It makes for a great homework piece. You can also coach the person through the pattern.

Exercise 4.4: Creating a new self narrative

Overview

1. Discover your story:
   a. "Up until now the story of my life has comprised a story of ..."
   b. "If I described the plot or theme of my life it would be ..."
   c. Complete the statement: "Up until now ... I thought, believed, felt, acted ..."
2. Step back from the story.
3. Find counter-examples.
4. Make up a new story that is more empowering.

Explain to the PWS that we understand our lives as *stories*. Because these stories may no longer serve you, you can choose to update them, edit them or otherwise "re-story" your life. Stop telling yourself the old blocking story and tell yourself a new one instead.

---

1. **Discover your story.**
   Ask the PWS some questions along the following lines:
   - What story have you been living up until now that contributes to your blocking?
   - Where did that story come from? Did someone give it to you? Did you make it up yourself?
   - Is the story part of your family story, your cultural story, your religious story, your racial story ...?
   - How much of the story did you personally adapt or create?
   - Tell about the theme of your life. What do you detect as the underlying narrative or pattern?
   - Does your narrative tell a story of victimhood or survival, of failing or winning, of connecting or disconnecting, of being rejected or of being loved and accepted ... ?
     a. **"Up until now the story of my life has comprised the story of ..."**
        (for example: a victim, a failure, bad luck, stress, rejection, ease, success, popularity, fame and so on)

     b. **"If I described the plot or theme of my life it would be ..."**
        (for example: a tragedy, a drama, a soap-opera, horror, melodrama, education plot, and so on)

     c. **Complete the statement:** *"Up until now ... I have thought, believed, felt, acted ..."*
        And then describe fully how you have responded mentally, emotionally, physically to your old story, in terms of your verbal behavior, the decisions you have made, the expectations you had and so on.

2. **Step back from the story.**
   - Evaluate the usefulness, productivity, value and emotional enjoyment of your story.
   - Would you recommend living in that story to anyone else?
   - How well has this narrative served you? What doesn't work very well or feel very good about that story?
   - Do you feel stuck simply because you do not know of *anything else* that you could possibly say about your experiences other than what you have already said?
   - Looking back at what happened, how else could you interpret those events in the light of what you know now?

3. **Find counter-examples.**

Most people have exceptions to their stories. For instance, most PWS have times when they are not living in fear and anxiety. Instead, they are relaxed and hence speak fluently. There are even occasions when they do not block in situations where they usually would. Indeed, one of the first things I do in working with PWS is to analyze those times when they are consistently fluent, because that proves that the PWS knows how to not block and stutter, and demonstrates to the PWS that they have the necessary resources and strategies for fluency. Then I elicit the structure of *how* they do that, how they operate from a state of calmness, courage, determination, comfort and focus – or even indifference!

Ask *how* questions. "How did you do that?"

- How did you not fall into anxiety and fear, but just keep at it?
- How did you resist losing your calmness, and communicate with your boss anyway?
- How did you not discount yourself in that instance?
- How did you prevent things from getting even worse with all of that happening?

4. **Make up a new story that is more empowering.**

Now think about how you would like your story to take you into the future:

"From this day on I will increasingly become more of a person who ..."

- Just for fun, make up a wild and rambunctious story. Use your imagination to its fullest capacity! Which positive and bright sparkling activities from your past could you really experience to the full? What kind of story would that be? Of course this may seem totally unrealistic, but you never know. Once you have experienced your dreams, you may want them to come true!

- Given this fantasy version of what could be, bring some of that sparkle into a more "reasonable" story. What would you like to grow into your new dominant story?

- What might be the consequences – both limiting and enhancing – of that?

If you need some inspiration for writing your new story, think of all the people you know who already demonstrate aspects of the story you would like your life to be:

- Whom do you know that you admire and appreciate?
- What story do they tell themselves about who they are, about others, the world ...?
- How could you have that for yourself?

You know how to tell stories, because you do it every day of your life! But now you are going to do it from the writer's (dissociated) point of view, which is objective, and has a clear intention. By objectifying your position you can see the events in your life as separate from you. You are outside of the problem, witnessing it, rather than directly experiencing it. Remember, you can only block when you are inside the state. By stepping outside you are in a position to study it, and to rewrite your story so that it turns out the way you would like it.

Chapter Five

Working with Stress

States of being

If I were to ask you what state of mind you are presently in, you could probably answer quite readily. Since you are reading this book, you may answer, "I am in a learning state." Or you may say, "I am in a curious state" or even, "I am in a state of confusion." You can usually give a name to the state of mind you are in at any given moment. Because "state" is hard to define precisely, we often use metaphors. We often talk about emotional states as though they are *liquids* which fill us up: "I'm full of admiration" or run dry: "I'm drained of pity". Emotions such as anger boil over, while love flows out.

You are always in some state of mind or emotion (unless you are dead), and this state of mind is in constant flux. Although many states are transitory – moments of exhilaration or dismay – some states may become habitual. What is your "usual" state? Are you generally grumpy, happy, tired, carefree, optimistic or energized ...?

Your state (whether anger, fear, anxiety, love, happiness ...) affects the way you interact with the world and other people. Each state influences the way you see, think, and feel, and thus your ability to communicate with others. Your ability to learn is governed by the particular state you are in at the time. You know from your own experience that if you are feeling bored or tired, or you have to take care of other people's needs, you are not going to be in the best state for paying attention to new information or thinking about how you can develop new ways of doing things.

Your physiological state, measured in terms of general arousal, can vary between coma to "up and at 'em" activity. Physiological and emotional states are related. For example, think of times when you were angry, anxious, curious, happy, attentive, confused, loving, and so on, and consider, "What does being in this state allow me to do – and not do?" You discover that your options vary a great deal. When you are in a state of high arousal you are more likely to experience certain kinds of emotional state and not others; it is hard to be under great stress and maintain a state of equanimity.

Getting the message

If you are experiencing a stressful state, your options are reduced. If you treat stress as a message from your body to your mind, it informs you that you need to take action to reduce your stress level. However, if the stress is producing fear and that is triggering a blocking response, taking effective action might be difficult. If fear initiates negative thinking, that is going to compound your inability to act appropriately.

Notice the kind of language that PWS use to amplify the blocking:

- "I'm blocking again!!"
- "I hate it when I stutter."
- "I can't go on doing this!"
- "If I stutter, they'll think I'm stupid."
- "Am I going to go on blocking for the rest of my life?"

I know that it usually isn't just this simple. Those old horror movies really are grooved into the muscles and run out of conscious awareness. Because they flow deeply, just talking to yourself using positive thinking will not fix them instantly. Yet by habitually talking to yourself in language that is positive and supportive, rather than beating yourself up, can produce remarkable and surprising results. Turning around what you say to yourself will change your behavior, but it will take a little time.

Dealing with stress

The time to learn state management skills, of course, is not during the stress storm. Learning navigation skills when a ship is tossing and turning in the open sea in the midst of 40 foot waves is a bit late in the game.

Michael Hall (1997)

Generally, when people are stressed, they are not in a good place for learning new strategies for changing their behavior. Under stress, people tend to revert to instinctive or habitual patterns, and these are often of the "fight, flight or freeze" variety. The PWS's usual response to stress is to freeze – then to start blocking. Therefore, by treating the freezing up as a signal, the PWS knows it is time to engage their *flow* response to this situation instead.

The way to manage your stress is to learn how to avoid sending the "Danger!" message when you encounter threats which are imaginary or irrational. Because the body-mind is hardwired to respond to any kind of threat, this is going to take some doing. It means learning to alter the meanings that you have given to certain events.

Having a conversation with someone is not usually a life threatening experience! You have to find a way to stop reacting as if it were, and to realize that in everyday conversations people are generally supportive and friendly. This means learning to respond more appropriately with your *adult* mind, maintaining state control, going with the flow, rather than reverting to the instinctive flight responses stemming from childhood hurts.

If you perceive a conversation as stressful, that tells you that you need to make some changes. One of those changes involves loving and honoring yourself no matter how you speak. Speaking is just talking. The fact is no one has ever died from blocking.

I asked some of my clients for their response to this idea. One replied:

> I think the real fear is that I am NOT going to die. If I died then I would not have to live out the shame and humiliation. I am not in a life threatening situation but I am in a *self-esteem threatening* situation. What is more painful, being totally humiliated or dying? At least dying will end my misery. But being humiliated seems never to end and it is a real threat. That is why it kicks the fight/flight

107

syndrome into action. Seriously, death is easy compared to living a life of humiliation. Sounds weird but ask any PWS how many times they wished they were dead. It is not the fear of death that activates the fight/flight mechanism it is the *fear of humiliation*. [Italics added]

Therefore start managing stress by raising your self-esteem and stopping thinking so much about other people's opinions of you. When you create new meanings of (reframe) the old triggers that produced blocking, there will be no need to become stressful, and you will be able to enjoy your conversations.

How to achieve relaxed alertness

To avoid the fear and anxiety emotions that set off blocking, the following *Flying Into Calm* pattern shows how you can learn to recognize the bodily symptoms of stress, to accept these as part of the normal functioning of the body, and to use various breathing, stretching and muscle relaxing exercises to achieve a state of calmness.

How can you become truly masterful in coping and handling the demands, challenges, threats, fears, and so on, of communicating at work and at home so that you don't stress out about these things? How can you?

Exercise 5.1: The *Flying Into Calm* Pattern

This is a self-help pattern for overcoming blocking.

Overview

1. Recognize the presence of stress.
2. Notice your strategy for stress
3. Practice *flying into calm.*
4. Find your calm state.

1. **Recognize the presence of stress.**
    You can only control or manage something effectively when you are aware of it. Therefore notice your bodily responses in those contexts which trigger the stress that initiates the blocking, and become aware of any stress in your body.

    Stress usually shows up in the body of a PWS as tightness in the throat, chest and jaw. The muscles tense in those areas and become inflexible. Now it may be that you have become so habituated to those stresses that at first the stress is not apparent. If you do not feel anything, you may find it useful to have some massage or bodywork sessions. Having gentle pressure applied to your body will let you know where you are holding the tension in your body – it will feel knotted up, and hurt a bit.

    Interpret the stress as a message from your body that you need to do something different. By communicating with the tension and tightness it can teach you. Be still and establish communication with that part of you responsible for causing the tightness and tension. Of course you can talk to parts of your body. Just try it, and notice what happens. (There is more below on talking to yourself.) Once you have introduced yourself – (Yes, I'm serious: say "Hello" to that part of you) – you could ask the tightness in your neck or in your chest:

    *   "What message do you have for me?"
    *   "What are you trying to do for me?"
    *   "What is the purpose of *tensing* in this way? Why have you *tightened* this part?"
        When you ask such questions, you will find that you do get answers forming in your mind. Heed them, whatever they are, even if they surprise you.

2. **Identify your strategy for stress.**
    What *physical elements* contribute to your stress or prevent you from operating from calmness?

    *   Shallow breathing.
    *   Tight throat and jaw.
    *   Poor posture.
    *   Contracted abdomen.
    *   Lack of focus; constant eye shifting.
    *   Tightening and holding neck muscles, pulling the head back.

It is also possible that you have emotional responses relating to these physical tensions in your body. It is as if the tension sets up pressures and needs requiring your attention. However, stress inhibits your ability to do this appropriately, and this then creates even more stress which can lead to impatience, frustration, and anger – which make calmness even further away.

- Does your stress have a feeling of *anger* in it?
- Does *impatience* contribute to your stress?
- How much does the desire to speak fluently contribute to your stress?

3. **Practice *flying into a calm*.**
People sometimes describe getting angry as "flying into a rage". With a strong trigger, people can fly into a rage at a moment's notice. Could you also fly into a state of worry, dread, and anxiety? Sure you can. Well, if you can do that, then you have already have the ability to do the opposite, and *fly into a calm*. Doing that would put you in an appropriate state for speaking fluently. Flying into a calm enables you to access a state of calm when you need it. Indeed, if you were to fly into a calm when you would normally expect the trigger to lead to blocking, that would eliminate the problem of stuttering.

Actually, I know you can already do this. You have experienced the "telephone voice" phenomenon. You know the scenario: you're in the middle of having an intense argument with a loved one. You're hearing things coming out of your mouth (and you're not blocking now!) or from that other person's mouth that they would never say to a stranger (they save those kinds of things for the people that they love most! It's their way of testing to see if you will keep on loving them if they do *this* to you!). So you are raising their voice, feeling really angry, upset, frustrated. and then the phone rings. You take a breath, pick up the phone, and then calmly and politely answer it. "Hello." You speak with a calm, professional telephone voice. The context suddenly changed and you instantly flew into a calm!

Creating a calm state

You may fly into a calm when by yourself, when speaking to a pet or to somebody you are comfortable with. Reflect on those times and ask yourself what enabled you to be calm, relaxed and speaking fluently. What beliefs, values, memories, decisions and attitudes go with that calm state and speaking so fluently? The answers will give you the mental frames of mind that permit you to fly into a calm. As these mental frames come to conscious awareness, trust your unconscious mind to give you even more reasons for you to fly into a calm in all situations.

Your ability to fly into a calm is already a resource; you only need to make it a key item in your repertoire. You probably need to practice, so that it becomes stronger, more powerful, and so that you can access it in a split second when you need it.

OK, I admit that for a person who blocks it may not be quite as simple as that in those extreme contexts where they go into a panic before speaking. However, let's not dismiss this process too soon. You may be surprised at what you can do. For sure, you have nothing to lose but some time practicing.

First, pay attention to that state of calm that you know you can achieve. Think about a time when you really demonstrated the power of your telephone voice (or something equivalent). Be there again, seeing what you saw, hearing what you heard, and feeling what you felt.

What enabled you to step out of the angry and yelling state to the calm and cool state where you said, "Hello!"? What beliefs, values, decisions, intentions empowered that response? Why didn't you answer the phone with your angry voice? Why didn't you yell at the person calling in? Your answers to these questions will help you identify the key aspects of how you can fly into a calm, so that you can generalize the strategy for use in other contexts in your life.

As you clarify each factor, amplify it to find the optimum value for best results. It is also important to establish a trigger – a word, a symbol, a special touch – that is associated with this ability to change your emotional state at will. In NLP this is called *anchoring* (see Bodenhamer and Hall, 1999, Chapter 13). Consider:

- What would be a good anchor or symbol for total calmness?
- What sound, sight, and sensation would remind me of this state?

Now practice stepping into it, setting that link to some trigger, breaking state, and then using the trigger to step back into that place where you manage your emotions.

4. **Finding your calm state.**
   Create your best representation of a confidently relaxed state. The best way to do this is to recall a time when you were really relaxed in a calm and centered way.

   Ask yourself:

   - What kind of relaxation do I need or want for speaking fluently in all contexts?
   - How can I feel calm and confident and relaxed whenever I speak?
   - What kind of a relaxed mind and emotions do I want or need in a given situation?

   Although you might think that their relaxed state involves lying on the beach on a sunny day, that is not really appropriate for the workplace or for those times that typically trigger blocking. A relaxed state is not about going limp or crashing out. There are other kinds of relaxation which would serve you better as a possible resource. You need to have a relaxed state which:

   - has the qualities of alertness, mindfulness, readiness, or whatever would make you resourceful when you typically block
   - gives you the sense that you are in control of the situation, that nothing will faze you or distract you from your purpose.

   Relaxed alertness means:

   - Your breathing is easy, you are no longer obsessing and your mind is at ease.

- You have a calm confidence in your ability to speak fluently, a relaxed attentiveness in listening fully to the other person.
- You are not concerned with whether or not he/she may be judging how you speak.
- It is also important that you can say "Yes" to being in this calm state (see Chapter Six).

The relaxed energy of readiness and eagerness to speak calmly gives you confidence because you are aware that your mind-body system knows how to perform optimally. It also means that when you are tested by life and slide into a block once in awhile, you are able to accept those everyday frustrations without judging yourself.

Imagine going to that place and associate totally into that experience. Recall this memory as richly as possible: see what you were seeing, hear what you were hearing, and feel what you were feeling – so that you can access this state. You may wish to amplify the state by making the pictures more vivid; by making the sounds more explicit; by talking to yourself in a calm relaxing way using words that totally and completely relax you. And then connect it to a code word, symbol, physical touch or sensation so that you have a ready access to that state. When you activate your code (fire your anchor), it will put you back into that calm state.

Once you have set this trigger, try it out for real by accessing this state just before entering a speaking engagement. Learn from what happens. Remember there is no "failure"; it's just a message that you need more practice. (For further information see Lederer & Hall, 1999). If you need to customize this set up, mentally step back and examine it, so that you can make any necessary adjustments. Find out what works best, and then amplify it, build your resource state:

- What is the nature and quality (pictures, sounds, feelings) of your relaxed state?
- What qualities and factors make up this state?
- What other qualities would you like to edit into this state?

Additional qualities

- For instance, you could add a big dose of healthy *humor* to the mix. The ability to lighten up, to not take your self or others so seriously, to enjoy people and experiences tremendously enriches relaxation. How many times have you become extremely fearful of a speaking moment when it was totally unnecessary? The people you were speaking to were not judging you like that and you know it. It was you who was doing the judging. Well, what about stepping outside that and seeing how ridiculous such thinking is. Could you now laugh at your childish behavior?

- You can explode most fears by *exaggerating* them. Go really over the top with the fear until it become ridiculous. Then exaggerate it some more; it becomes ludicrous. Your sense of humor enables you to operate in a more humble and delightful way.

- How about *appreciation*? What if you moved through the world appreciating things, people, and experiences more? Instead of fearing what other people may think of your speech, *appreciate* that most will listen patiently to you. Appreciate that you can not only speak, but you can in some contexts speak fluently. I know some mute people who would love to have those abilities.

- *Magnanimity* is another resource. It would enable you to operate from a sense of a having a big heart and thereby prevent you from becoming mentally ruffled. How would that enhance your life?

- You could choose to be *open*, to *accept what the world offers you*. You could be more *flexible, forgiving, playful, balanced* ... the list goes on and on. Create you own set of resourceful qualities that will enhance your core relaxation state. Practice, practice, practice building that state so that instead of flying into a block you fly into a calm.

Defusing emotions

Emotions have a profound effect on whether or not the PWS blocks and stutters. The PWS can learn how to control those emotions which have got out of perspective. In Chapter Two it was proposed that people evaluate their experience based on their expectations of what happens next, they learn to associate their emotions with whether or not their experience of the world matches those expectations.

The degree of association can change. The adult mind can judge which emotions are appropriate for a particular experience. Most inappropriate emotions are linked to the past, possibly childhood experiences. A PWS may claim that because "I was scared of my father because every time I started stuttering he would yell, 'Spit it out! Spit it out!' and ever since then I have been afraid of authority figures for they will want me to 'spit it out' and I can't. That's why I stutter." This kind of generalization needs to be challenged; the PWS needs to sort out these confusions, as there is no need to hang on to the embarrassments from childhood and apply them to present situations. For example, the person they are talking to now is *not* that yelling parent, that threatening or ridiculing authority figure. It's time for the PWS to make new evaluations about their emotional responses as the old ones are no longer justified.

Exercise 5.2: The *Emotions Are Just Signals* Pattern

Emotions have a profound effect on whether or not the PWS blocks and stutters. The PWS needs to know how to control those emotions which have got out of hand. The following exercise provides several ways to reframe those negative emotions.

Overview

1. Recognize that emotions are just signals.
2. Access a witnessing state.
3. Recognize the triggers that evoke the blocking
4. Say to yourself, "It is just an emotion."
5. Give yourself permission to change the meaning that drives the emotion.
6. Use a positive resource.
7. Check alignment.
8. Put into your future and install.

1. **Recognize that emotions are just signals.**
   Remind the PWS that their emotions are there for a purpose, which is to help them evaluate and decide whether or not their experience is enjoyable and worth pursuing. In this sense it is information about their relationship with an experience. The point is: are they acting on that information unthinkingly, or are they engaging in a proper evaluation of what is happening?

2. **Access a witness state to one of the major negative emotions around blocking.**
   Ask the PWS to name one of the emotions they associate with blocking. It could be *fear, anxiety, confusion, anger,* or whatever. Have them take a deep breath and then release it as they mentally step back from that negative emotion. They need to be far enough away to witness – objectively observe – that emotion.

   Say to the PWS: "Know that this negative emotion offers an evaluation of your current experience and your model of the world."

   Ask the following questions:

   • "What was going on in your life when you created this emotion?"
   • "What should you have expected from that time? Should you have expected any other reaction or anything different?"

   Many PWS have told me they can tell just by looking that other people think it funny to hear them block and stutter: they may snicker, seem embarrassed, not know what to do. Ask, "What do you expect?"

   If you had never heard or seen someone block and stutter, and then when they try to speak to you they lock up in a block, how do you expect you would react? Perhaps with the laughter of embarrassment? The majority of people do not intend to make fun of you. Some may feel sympathetic toward you, some may even feel empathy – they feel your hurt, they struggle with you as they see you struggle. Even if someone makes fun of you, whose problem is it? It is only your problem if you make it so.

   Once the PWS has answered your question about their expectations, get them to evaluate what they have said in terms of whether or not it is logical or reasonable. The fact that you are asking them to witness their own thoughts suggests that they need to consider their answer, and decide how appropriate it is.

3. **Recognize the triggers that evoke the blocking.**
    Discuss the following questions with the PWS:

    *   "Where do you block worst? What is going on when you block?"
    *   Step back from those times of blocking and note what is going on that triggers the fear and anxiety, those negative emotions that cause you to freeze up and block.
    *   "Knowing that you do not always block, that in certain situations [name them] you are fluent, what has to happen in order for you to experience fear and anxiety and then block?"
    *   "What do you have to see, hear or feel in order for you to know that it is time to block?"
    *   If it is a feeling: a) what emotion is behind the feeling? b) what thought is behind that emotion? and c) what triggers that thought?
    *   "Does the interpretation you are putting on the events that trigger you to block accurately represent what is happening? Or are you responding to some old learning from childhood that is no longer relevant today? If so, know that that emotion is *just* an emotion.

4. **Say to yourself: "It's *just* an emotion."**
    Lead the PWS to use their most resourceful voice to say something like, "I am more than my emotions. I experience emotions, but I am more than just my emotions." It is OK for them to put this in their own words. It is vital that the PWS be able to separate their *identity* from their *emotions* as this is a vital step towards their learning how to control their state. Then ask them:

    *   "If that emotion is just information, what does it tell you that will help you change what you do?"

    Ask them to consider:

    *   "Who is in control here? You or your emotions? Who's running the show?"

117

Suggest that they refuse to treat their emotions as being the final arbiter, or as providing a final report on their standing, status, destiny and identity. Instead, "Decide to *learn* from your emotions, treat them as signals and messages about the relationship between your perception of the world at the particular moment when you generated the emotion. Keep the emotion to the context in which it originated. Do not let it color your life."

5. **Give yourself permission to change the meaning that drives the emotion.**
   Ask the PWS to go inside and make appropriate changes to anything that is no longer useful.

   - "Go inside and give yourself permission to change the meaning of this emotion. Should any internal objection come up, welcome it, find out what its intention for you is, and find another way of satisfying it. (See step 7 for reframing any objecting parts.)

   - "What new meanings for that emotion will permit you to minimize its effect?"

   For example:

   - "I learned this emotion when I was being made fun of as a child for my stuttering. I am no longer a child. I am an adult and I can handle anyone who thinks it is clever to make fun of me today. They have the problem – not me!"
   - "I give myself permission to feel fear because it allows me to recognize things that are a true threat to me and to take appropriate action early."
   - "I give myself permission to feel the tender emotions because it makes me more fully human."

6. **Use a positive resource.**
   Ask the PWS to find a resource which will override that negative emotion and minimize or eliminate its power.

   - "Which resourceful state could you use to override that negative emotion, and would minimize or eliminate its power."

"You may like to consider this list of resourceful states: calmness, courage, faith, persistence, determination, being centered."

"Access the resource state that you choose and then find a way of amplifying to make it even more powerful. Then, holding this resource state, allow it to overpower the negative emotion that you do not want. Feel this sense of calmness, courage, faith ... [use their actual words] permeating the whole of your being, and replacing that unwanted emotion with this positive resource state."

"Meta-State the negative emotion with your positive emotion as you apply the positive emotion to the negative emotion."

7. **Check alignment.**
    You need to check with the PWS that they are totally aligned with this change. If there is a part of them that objects to this change, that part could sabotage this process and kick the person right back into the negative emotion.

    Therefore, go inside, and ask if there are any parts of you which have any objections to the proposed change.

    •   "Does any part of you object to letting this operate as your primary style in dealing with this emotion?"

    You may need to make a list. After each objection ask, "Are there any more parts which object?" If so, go back to step 5.

    The next step is to find out each part's intention – its higher purpose – so that it may be satisfied in a more appropriate way. In NLP it is presupposed that all behavior has a positive intent. That is not to say that the intent is ethically or morally correct. The intent relates to the circumstances at the time and the resources the person had available.

    A frequently asked question concerning this presupposition is, "What about a person who sexually abuses a child? What is the positive intent behind that?" Most abusers were abused themselves; the adult's behavior, however horrible, could be an unconscious attempt on the part of the adult to experience love

119

or even to give it. This may seem sick – and it is – but it is true to experience. Having worked with several abusers I found that such intents are common. Part of the person wants something which is currently denied them. Having very few strategies available, *anything* might be better than doing nothing.

A PWS was dealing with her fear of giving up stuttering. It is a major issue with her. The intent or purpose of her stuttering is that it serves as a means of stopping her from being successful. Because if she were successful in her career then she would be going out and meeting new people, traveling the country and even the world giving presentations. Although she is a superb, fluent public speaker when in her empowerment state, she knows that is a problem because to her, being successful means she will be "out there" and being "out there" means that she is in danger. So she retains her stuttering behavior to protect her from this danger, which is (a) *failure* and (b) *the possibility of getting hurt*. Indeed, the word she used to describe that fear of success was "terror." So the part of her which has the intention of keeping her safe needs to maintain the stuttering because that will prevent her from being successful and thus will protect her from failure and being hurt. Paradoxically, staying safe means continuing to stutter – and that causes more failure and more hurt. The person thus experiences incongruence – they are at odds with themselves; their behavior doesn't get them what they want.

When working with these kinds of issues, it is important to generalize to elicit the higher positive intents of those objecting parts which are rooted in hurt. Have the PWS associate fully into the objecting part before questioning it. The more they feel the part, the easier for the unconscious mind to provide answers. It is simple to do. Just ask the person:

* "What is the purpose or intention of that part?"
* "What is it trying to do for you?"
* "What does that part want for you that is important?"
* "What would that part have to give up which is important to you in order for you to align your life with this higher intent?" This question elicits the secondary gain of the behavior. They will need to find another means of achieving that intent before the part will allow the change.

This line of questioning will get you the higher positive intent. Just keep repeating these questions until you reach something really positive (and very abstract). Once you have found this overall mission, ask the person to find a more acceptable way to achieve it without the negative emotions. Tell the PWS to let that part know that as an adult they now have the ability to protect themselves from harm without having the negative emotion. By telling them that they now have adult resources for protection, you are in effect reframing the objecting part.

How could my client protect herself from the fear of failure and from being hurt without stuttering? Well, when she is living in her "empowered state" (which is a powerfully religious state) she feels safe and protected and there is no fear of failure. She then needs to apply this state widely to other aspects of her life.

8. **Put into your future and install.**
   Finally check that the change will hold. Ask the person to imagine themselves in the future living with the benefit of the new resources.

   - "Given that you have now got rid of those inappropriate emotions, how will your life be different in the future?"
   - "By leaving those old emotional evaluations in your childhood where they belong, how will it be moving into the future?"
   - "Is this an appropriate way for you to move through the world?"
   - "Imagine these new resources supporting you in the future. How is that for you? Do you need to make any adjustments?" Continue to add resources until the person is satisfied with their future way of being.

Having the means for dealing with stress is of utmost importance for the PWS because for them stress is an ever-present reality. Learning to fly into a calm, with a more appropriate set of emotional responses is a significant step towards fluency.

Chapter Six

Techniques of Change

Frames

The particular meaning we make of experience comes from the way we perceive our reality. Meaning depends upon our present need and our past experience. A *frame* is that way of perceiving the world. For example, if you are looking for a birthday present for a friend, your perceptual frame will influence the way you shop, and relate to your knowledge of that person and your expectations of what they will like. This book has a Blocking and Stuttering frame in that it pays attention to some of the available information about this topic and ignores other topics. There is a predominant focus on a certain kind of behaviour: how the PWS responds to particular situations and people, and how to change that response.

The frames you put around any behavior critically determine your responses. Every frame slants your interpretation of events, and will be more or less useful for achieving a particular objective. Therefore you need to develop the ability to shift frames at will as part of running your own mind and managing your own states. To change the meaning of some event or some behavior, adopt an alternative frame or mode of perception.

Reframing – changing your mind

Because every frame is a biased and partial perception of reality, it is always possible to change the bias and see things from a different point of view. *Reframing* changes the meaning of an experience. You reframe your understanding by seeing things from a different point of view. An oft-quoted example is that of the half-filled glass of water: is it half-empty or half-full? The glass of water stays the same; the frame of mind you have alters the meaning. This book could be said to be about reframing the meanings the PWS have placed around blocking and stuttering. By removing the negative associations to blocking and stuttering, the PWS finds it possible to regain fluency. Instead of responding to a situation with anxiety about their performance, they come to see this as an opportunity for expressing something important about themselves. The PWS adopts a more optimistic state of mind, putting greater trust in their body to perform well they can concentrate more on the content of what they have to say and monitor the responses they are getting from the other person.

Whatever the behavior, it is the meaning you give it that influences your state, your emotional response, and your potentiality for taking action. In every case I have worked with or know about, the PWS invariably sees blocking as something *bad* to be *avoided*. Given that meaning, they inevitably *fear* blocking. The act of fearing blocking creates the blocking. To become fluent the PWS has to release the old meanings they have associated with blocking and stuttering; the challenge for them is find new meanings which will serve them. The good news is that there are many ways of doing this.

How reframing works

A point of view is just a point of view. However, some points of view provide interpretations of experience that enable more useful and effective interventions. There are always alternative points of view available to you; you are frequently changing your perception and understanding of the world. For example, think of how your attitude towards a famous sports star changes when they miss a vital goal, or you discover that they have been taking performance enhancing drugs, cheating on their partner, and so on. Although you know there are options, the mind cannot actually entertain two different points of view simultaneously. Remember the picture of the Old Hag/Young Woman (Figure 3.3). You see one or the other, but not both simultaneously. Only one thing at a time, even though you know it could be otherwise.

This chapter deals with the conscious reframing of blocking. Although reframing may occur naturally, NLP offers some systematic ways of deliberately changing the meaning of experience, and thus leads to a change in behavior. One way to do that is to turn around the language someone uses. You could think:

- "What would be a more useful way of putting this?"
- "What would be the opposite of that?"

For example, reframe the statement:

- "If I block, people will judge me as being an inadequate person."

by changing it to:

- "If people judge me as being inadequate if I block, that is their problem. My sense of self-worth comes from how I view myself and not from what others may or may not think of me."

This example of reframing changes the locus of control. You put yourself in charge rather than anyone else dictating how they think you should be.

This is a good example of the need for updating childhood maps. The PWS can identify and then reframe those old childhood beliefs. They need to deliberately do this at first, until it becomes natural. For example, they can reframe the belief "I am a weirdo for blocking" by thinking:

- "No way! I am nothing of the kind! I learned that behavior as a child. Now that I am an adult I realize that I am far more than just a 'behavior'. And being an adult who is constantly learning, I am in the process of conquering this behavior."

- "No, it may have seemed to some that I was a weirdo for blocking, but if they go on thinking that, then that is their problem. They are only seeing a part of me, and they need to be more adult."

- "I am far more than just a person with a challenging behavior. I am a kind person. I am a loving person. I am resourceful and caring. I am in charge of my life."

Changing meaning by reframing

NLP describes two basic ways to reframe meaning: Context Reframing and Content Reframing.

Context reframing asks: "*Where* would this be really useful and valuable?" to find alternative contexts in which the experience could be useful. An example of context reframing would be: "Where could this *fear* that I have around blocking be useful?" "I sure don't need that kind of fear when speaking, but if I am in physical danger of losing my life, that fear could save me."

You might be wondering in which contexts stuttering would be useful. Well, there are some comedians (Michael Palin in the movie, *A Fish Called Wanda*; Ronnie Barker in the UK sitcom *Open All Hours*) who have created comedic characters who stutter – though you probably have your own views on whether it is OK to poke fun at stuttering. It is conceivable that stuttering could be a way of buying time to think or delay making a decision. Actually, context reframing is not the one to concentrate on.

Content reframing asks: "*What else* could this mean?" to find other meanings for the experience or behavior (the three examples above are content reframes). So that while everything remains objectively the same, the meaning of the behavior is interpreted from another point of view and this then offers an alternative strategy for intervening to change things. For example, the behavior of stuttering or blocking could mean:

- "I'm just giving myself time to think."
- "I just love certain sounds so much that I repeat them to myself."
- "I like to keep my audience in suspense so that they pay more attention."

Content reframing changes the belief "If I block, I am weak" to "If I block, that is an opportunity for finding out more about myself and to test my strength and ability to change." You alter your response to your perception of the conditions in which stuttering used to occur (that's another way of reframing – treat it as though it happened in the past). A content or meaning reframe is essentially saying, "Although X can mean Y, it can also mean Z, and Z is better in some way."

Reframing the situation

The PWS has already had much practice in identifying the initial conditions, the triggers or cues that let them know, "It's time to stutter." The actual external events are going to stay the same; what changes is the way the PWS perceives them. People come to associate a particular meaning to a particular event. They create numerous simple correspondences between what happens and their responses. For example, they meet an authority figure and respond in a certain way. Their story tells them to become apprehensive, to get away, or to feel guilty. No one makes them have that response; it is something they have learned to do. By rewriting the story, they can change those limiting responses, and find new associations that serve them better. In other words, by reframing the situation their behavior changes. So how do they do this?

If you perceive the other person as an "authority figure", then consider that, for example:

- "Your 'authority' only resides in a particular area of your life. There are other areas where you see me as an authority. I am an authority figure too – on stuttering! – and many other things besides."
- "If you are in a position of power, then you have the wisdom to know how to treat me with the respect I deserve!"

Other people are not authority figures all of the time. Just imagine them engaging in the mundane activities which everyone does when they are "off-duty": putting out the garbage, shopping in the supermarket, sitting on the toilet. You are only limited by your imagination.

Alternatively, you could stand back from the whole situation, and observe what is going on. From this witness position you might conclude that:

- the stuttering is a message that you have not yet got your ideas sorted, that you're paying attention to the wrong end of the communication loop; that the way you present yourself, in terms of posture (where you're looking, how you are standing, breathing, and so on) and your manner of speaking (your voice tonality needs to vary much more, to be brighter ...) could do with a makeover.
- stuttering is a great way of dominating a conversation. The longer you stutter the more you are the one in control. This changes the value of the PWS's commonly perceived lowly status.

Those reframes address the initial conditions. Consider your responses:

- "What would need to happen to make the stuttering response boring, trivial, or unworthy of your attention?"
- "What would happen if you absolutely did not care if you blocked and stuttered?"

The response usually is something like this, "Well, I wouldn't stutter." This question simply asks the person to change the meaning of blocking as something bad, feared and to be avoided to something not all that significant. We can say this with certainty – those who overcome blocking cease giving so much negative meanings to those times when they do block or even stumbling with words a little bit. Everyone has those times of stumbling.

Working with reframes can be great fun as well as therapeutic! Most jokes are reframes; the PWS ought to be rolling around on the floor if you do this exercise thoroughly!

Ask the PWS to come up with as many meaning reframes as possible: "What else could this mean that would be useful?" Asking the PWS to use *their* imagination to find positive reframes usually works better than the clinician providing them. They already have the imagination; they just need to direct it differently. In this way the PWS takes responsibility for their own cure. The presupposition is that the person has the answers to their own healing within their existing resources, and that by bringing them into the foreground they are already on the path to success.

Reclaiming your power: Case Study 6

The following is a transcript of a session with Sally (see Chapter Two) who was experiencing the feeling of great tightness around her throat when speaking to other people. This tightness was especially strong when she was in a social situation.

"So, Sally, when you are in a social situation, you really feel tightness around your throat?"

"Yes."

"And what does the tightness mean to you?"

"Terror!"

"So, behind the tightness is terror?"

"Yes. Oh, yes. I am terrified of speaking to other people. Whenever I am in a social situation and even think of speaking, I become terrified."

"Does speaking to other people have any other meanings to you?"

"I want to remain invisible. I don't want anyone to see me."

"What are you terrified of, Sally?"

"I am afraid I will stutter."

"So when you speak to other people you become terrified that you will stutter and you want to be invisible? What is there about speaking to other people that causes you to choose to be terrified of stuttering and want to be invisible?"

"Everyone will be uncomfortable. They will not want to talk to me. They may not like me."

"Oh, I see. So you are afraid that the other people will become uncomfortable with your stuttering and because of their being uncomfortable, they will not want to talk to you?"

"Yes, that is correct."

"Tell me, how do you know that they may not like you?"

"Stuttering sounds bad. Everybody knows that. And people judge you by how you look and how you talk?"

"Oh, they do? *Everyone* judges you by how you look and how you talk?"

"Of course. Sure they do."

"Have you asked them? How many people have told you that in the last few years?"

"Well, I haven't asked everyone, but everybody knows you are judged by how you look and how you talk." (Sally was adamant about holding onto that belief of other people judging her primarily by how she talked.)

"Sally, how come you want to be invisible? How long have you wanted to be invisible?"

"I have wanted to be invisible ever since I was a little girl."

"What was that about? How come you wanted to be invisible as a little girl?"

"As a little girl, I was afraid to open my mouth or mother would get mad. She was always critical of me. She never complimented me. Mother was a witch. She looked like a witch. I can see her face now."

"You were afraid to speak or your mother would get mad? She even looked like a witch?"

"Yes, I can see her face now."

"What do you feel when you see your mother's face?"

"I feel that tightening around my throat. It is like a rope choking me."

"So you were afraid to speak up in your home and you wanted to be invisible?

"Yes, mom and dad fought all the time. I remember momma with a knife trying to kill dad. They were running around and dad begged her to put the knife away. I was afraid momma would kill me. I wanted to be invisible."

"You have a movie in your mind of your mother trying to kill your dad and you were afraid she would kill you?"

"Yes, and it terrified me."

"So, we sure know where much of that terror comes from. Where do you feel that terror in your body?"

"In my jaw."

There is enough information there to know where Sally learned to be fearful of speaking. Growing up in that terribly dysfunctional family, Sally learned that to survive it was best for her to remain quiet and invisible. Not mentioned above were comments about her father. Her dad also was critical of her. She never could be good enough for him. From her mother and father, Sally learned to be fearful of the judgments of other people.

Importantly, Sally embodied the emotions from the childhood trauma in her throat and in her jaw. In other words, her blocking was an attempt to remain invisible and to avoid judgment. As a result of therapy – which took a number of sessions over several months to complete – Sally has let those fears go and now speaks with much greater fluency. During those sessions we used many of the techniques described in this book. As a result, Sally has become much more resourceful, and has a very healthy and strong sense of self-esteem which permits her to disregard the judgments of others.

Blocking as avoidance

When relating to others, PWS often think: "I'll avoid any situations around people or groups that will attract attention to me and expose this weakness." "If I am around people I will try to cover up or block the stuttering so that I don't look foolish." This attitude demonstrates negatively stated (away from) outcomes (see Exercise 3.3). Negative outcomes or desires tend to create even more fear and start a spiral of negative thinking. Reframing breaks this vicious spiral. The art is to restate the intention in positive terms (Figure 6.1):

Original list from the case study:	Alternative (positive, towards):
I am not going to attract attention to myself.	I want to focus attention on …
I am not going to let others see my vulnerabilities.	I am going to show people my strengths.
I will not give others the chance to laugh at me.	I can laugh at myself.
I will not let them see me struggle.	I want other people to treat me with respect.
I will try to cover the stuttering up.	Only by being open will I be able to change.

Figure 6.1: Positive reframes

If it appears the PWS is avoiding things, you could confront them with one of the reframes in the list below. Otherwise, the standard question to ask when the PWS makes a negative statement is: "OK, so that's what you don't want. What do you want instead?" By stating the opposite, the person is confronted by congruency issues. Simply saying the opposite, as in "I want other people to treat me with respect" will bring up other potential issues that need to be resolved.

Reframing such beliefs requires the PWS to step outside their limiting belief frame and to consider alternatives. This is a fourth position activity, and it should be fun to do! (For further information on this, see Hall & Bodenhamer 2001, Chapter 6). Here are some more examples of how you can reframe a PWS's statements about themselves:

Reframing outcome/purpose statements

I am not going to attract attention to myself.

- "Actually most people want to grab other people's attention. What makes you so different?"
- "So I should ignore you?"
- "So you're not worth paying attention to?"
- "What would happen if you did?" "What would happen if you didn't?"

I am not going to let others see my vulnerabilities.

- "Why, where do you keep them? In a safe at home?"
- "How do you know that you are vulnerable? Who decided that?"
- "If I had that belief, I would have never left my parent's home for I sure am vulnerable!"
- "What would happen if you 'celebrated' your vulnerabilities and joined the human race?"

I will not give others the chance to laugh at me.

- "But can you laugh at yourself?"
- "Comedians work hard to get people to laugh at them."
- "If someone laughs at you because you block and stutter, who really has a problem, you or them? They just need to grow up, don't they?"
- "In the past year, how many people have laughed at you because of your blocking and stuttering?" "Did you join in?"

I will not let them see me struggle.

- "You'd better hide under a blanket then."
- "You have struggled most of your life with this problem. Have you ever considered just letting the struggling go and just relax with an attitude of 'I don't care if they see me struggle or not'? If they have a problem with it, it is their problem."

I will avoid any situations around people or groups that will expose this weakness.

- "So it's the hermit's life for you then."
- "You mean, you don't want to practice getting better?"
- "What do you mean by the term 'weakness'?"
- "That sure is weak thinking, isn't it?"

I will try to cover the stuttering up.

- "Go on then. Show me how you do that." "Don't 'try' – just do it."
- "You mean, you have nothing worth saying?"
- "How about covering up that kind of thinking?"
- "And when you do that, what happens?"
- "Wouldn't it be better to just admit the obvious and go ahead and just talk the best you could?"

Patterns for increasing self-esteem

[Adapted from the original by L. Michael Hall PhD (Hall, 1996, 2000, pp. 81–2).]

Accepting self-acceptance and appreciating self-appreciation

Because most PWS have low opinions of themselves, they need ways of boosting their confidence if they are to develop greater fluency. They need to stop identifying their sense of identity with a particular speech behavior and to accept and appreciate themselves more. This section considers what would happen to their speech if instead of identifying their blocking *behavior* with their sense of *self* they accepted and appreciated themselves as worthwhile people regardless of any stuttering?

We can identify three aspects of esteem:

- *Accepting* who you are, "warts and all".
- *Appreciating* what you do, acknowledging what you are good at.
- *Awe* for what you have the potential to become, what you aspire to.

One way of developing your self-worth is based on an interpretation of the 3Ps that Seligman refers to in his work on Learned Helplessness (see Chapter Two):

The first P is *Personal*, and relates to personal identity. This is where you need to demonstrate *Acceptance*.

> Acceptance is about noticing your various qualities, whatever you judge them to be, and simply accepting "This is how I appear to be now." "This is just one way of describing who I am." You accept who you are without hiding anything, without going into denial, without pretending that everything is "just fine". Just as there are always some personal qualities people do not like about themselves, there is always room for improvement, and a lifetime for doing it. There would be little point in living if you were "perfect".

The second P is for the *Pervasiveness* of Behavior, and this is where you need *Appreciation*.

> Every person has a number of skills they perform well without really thinking about them. You may consider them "ordinary" or "trivial" simply because for you they are no big deal. For example, you may be a great cook, love gardening, or find satisfaction in balancing the accounts. You might think "doesn't everybody do this?" but the truth is, they don't. Other people lacking those particular talents may admire your capability.

The third P relates to your way of thinking that your model of the world is *Permanent*, and this is where you need to develop a sense of *Awe* about what you can become!

> Every human being has a reason for living. Some think of this as their mission or purpose. Whatever the label, this notion is about becoming all that you might possibly become in your spiritual journey, in fulfilling your potential as a human being. And when you think about the richness of your life experience, this inspires a sense of awe and wonder, as you realize how much there can be … and there is even more than that!

Acceptance, Appreciation & Awe/Esteem Pattern

I have already mentioned that the primary goal for the speech pathologist in working with the PWS is to assist them in building up a healthy self-esteem that will allow them to feel sufficiently good about themselves so that caring whether they stutter becomes irrelevant. Once they release that concern, fluency improves. Consider the meaning frames I have elicited from PWS: "If PWS really feel good about themselves both when they are fluent and when they stutter, would blocking and stuttering have such negative meanings to them? If those negative meanings weren't there, would they block and stutter?" The vast majority would not. Therefore, building up a resourceful self is imperative for the PWS.

In Chapter Two I mentioned how people layer their thoughts and lock the original thought in with judgments, opinions, conditions, and so on. Usually the PWS does this in a negative way, laying negative thought on top of negative thought. This has a multiplying effect on their fear and anxiety, and makes the block harder to shift. However, you can utilize the same kind of thinking but have it work for you by changing the nature of the thoughts you add. By building layers of positive thoughts and resources, and by applying them to their concept of their self the positive multiplying effect creates an even more empowered person.

Exercise 6.1: Increasing self-esteem

The purpose of the Self-Esteem pattern is to make sure the PWS has three kinds of powerful resources that will change the way they respond to those situations that used to lead to blocking.

Overview

1. Access resource state for each **A**: *Acceptance, Appreciation, Awe.*
2. Amplify each state and apply to your concept of self.
3. Identify a needed context for greater self-esteem.
4. Apply your powerful self-esteeming state where it is needed.
5. Imagine a new future.
6. Personal ecology check.

Figure 6.2: Accessing resources

1. **Access a resource state for each *A*.**

   Access each state by remembering an occasion on which you were able to accept, appreciate or be in awe of something about yourself (Figure 6.2). Find a code or word for each of those states, so that you can access the state again when you choose.

   Acceptance – Remember a time when you were able to accept something that challenged you: perhaps someone mentioned one of your personal qualities that you had not been aware of, or acknowledged one of your skills that you had been taking for granted. When you thought about it, you were able to accept that truth about yourself at that time.

   Appreciation – Think of something that you do naturally and well, which you really appreciate as one of your talents. Are you proud of your family, your home, your work? All around you is evidence of your positive achievements. Feel the glow of self-appreciation and anchor that.

   Awe – Think of the range of your potential as a human being – all the things you aspire to, that you desire to become, that you stand in awe of. What is there that just blows your mind because it is so awesome? I look up at the night sky and contemplate its vastness and its mystery; I listen to great music in awe and become immersed in its complexity and beauty.

2. **Amplify the three states and *apply* each of them to your concept of *self*.**

   Amplify each state in turn so that it is robust enough to apply to your sense of self. Think of your *self* as meaning who you are as a unique person having your own life experiences, desires and capabilities. You can amplify the qualities of a state by making your image of it more colorful, bigger, brighter, and so on. Use positive and empowering language to support a strong sense of *acceptance, appreciation* and *awe/esteem.*

Activate each amplified resource in turn, and be fully in it. You could imagine stepping into a resource bubble and allowing it to permeate your whole being; or you could imagine your resource radiating from a source deep inside you, filling your whole body and even the space around you. In this way you have a stronger self-concept available for *accepting, appreciating* and *esteeming* more of yourself.

Apply these resources one at a time to your sense of self, to who you are (Figure 6.3). Just get a thought of yourself and apply each resource to that thought. You are meta-stating yourself using these three resource states. For example, I can just think of myself as "Bob" and then *apply* those states to that sense of "Bob". "I *accept* Bob", "I *appreciate* Bob", and, "I stand in *absolute amazement, awe* and *esteem* of Bob." It actually brings tears to my eyes every time I do it. This pattern asks you to love yourself. If that is a novel idea for you, go ahead and do it anyhow, even if you have to force yourself to do it!

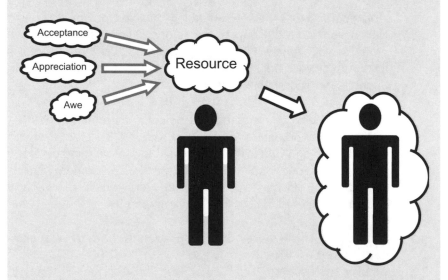

Figure 6.3: Increasing self-esteem

There are several ways of applying resource states. For example, you could first get into a resourceful state, and then being in that step into and merge with that other you. Or you could be in observer or fifth position and beam the resources to yourself, onto *that you over there*. Then step into that you and facing that higher self, accept those resources into your being.

Having applied your three resources of acceptance, appreciation and awe to your sense of self, you are now more personally empowered and ready to imagine yourself fully charged up in another context where this resource would be useful.

3. **Identify a needed context for applying these three resources.**
   Decide in what context you would prefer a more resourceful response. Choose one of those situations where your self-esteem used to go into the gutter and where the blocking was particularly in evidence. This could be a context where you were inclined to feel self-contempt, question your own nature, doubt your abilities, or dislike yourself.

4. **Apply your powerful self-esteeming state where it is needed.**
   Imagine seeing yourself in a comparable future "needy" situation and apply your new resourceful state from step 2 to that you, allowing your acceptance, appreciation and awe to transform that situation. Your point of view shifts as you associate into that other as you fully accept all the resources you now have available. Notice how this transforms the old context. Experience yourself now with this new sense of self-acceptance, self-appreciation and self-esteem.

5. **Imagine a new future.**
   Imagine moving fully resourced through life in the weeks and months to come. Your life will be different because you have those resourceful states available to you. Put yourself in some typical situations where in the past you would have started blocking. Notice how you are now more fluent. Be aware of any further improvements you could make in the way you speak.

Doing this limits the amount of power others can have over you. Esteeming yourself means you care less about what others think about how you talk, and that allows you to care more for those people. You are better able to accept, appreciate and esteem them because you accept, appreciate and esteem yourself.

139

6. **Personal ecology check.**
Are all parts of you aligned with this new concept of yourself? If so, welcome that and thank yourself. If there is a part of you which is not OK with the new arrangement, find that part's purpose for you and obtain its permission to let you think enough about yourself so that you will not allow what you *think* others may think of you to control how you speak. (See Exercise 5.2, step 7 for dealing with objecting parts.)

Become aware over the next period of weeks or months how your personal power or self-respect increases.

The Swish Pattern

The Swish Pattern is a way of replacing the strategy you don't want with a more appropriate strategy that leads to fluency. Use this process for changing your response to an event that triggers the blocking behavior. Making a new connection takes only a little practice; your substituted response will be activated automatically by the inciting incident. You could see it as rewiring the old stimulus-response linkage. The Swish process works by sending the unwanted response movie off into the background and replacing it with a more useful and desirable one. If this sounds familiar, it is because this pattern is similar to the Foreground/Background Pattern covered in Chapter Three. The Swish Pattern is powerful because you are installing a new behavioral response, and thereby moving toward the kind of person you want to become.

You can design swishes for yourself that set your mind, emotions, speech and behavior in a direction which aligns with your life purpose. Be drawn toward an image of yourself that is more valued, esteemed, loved, competent, happy, energetic and kind. This is a change of direction for people who block because they have developed the habit of seeing themselves experiencing blocking in their very next conversation. The Swish pattern retrains their mind to go beyond blocking, to even go beyond a concern for fluency, so that they can become all that they are inspired to be, so that they may be in awe of their personal capabilities and achievements.

Exercise 6.2: The Swish Pattern

In using the Swish Pattern, start by being fully associated into the old pattern. Then you can be pulled toward the new outcome image of the resourceful you. Many people find it is preferable to close their eyes during the process and open them between steps. Discover what works best for you.

Overview

1. Identify experience to be changed.
2. Clarify the internal movie of this experience.
3. Develop a desired outcome picture.
4. Link the two representations.
5. Swishing the pictures.
6. Swish five times.
7. Test.

1. **Identify experience to be changed.**
   Re-access your usual movie of fearing you will block in your very next conversation. Make sure that you are associated in this movie. If you are seeing yourself in the picture that means you are dissociated, so actually be in yourself, looking out through you own eyes in the picture, seeing what is around you.

   Notice: What are you aware of just before you block? What do you see, hear, and feel that initiates your fear or anxiety of blocking? Make sure you have a sufficiently detailed Image of that situation.

2. **Clarify the internal movie of this experience.**
   You may be unaware of what exactly the trigger is for blocking. It is as if you have been on automatic pilot to some extent and the pattern operates out of habit. You can bring into awareness some of the cues by testing for key elements in the movie which create the fear of blocking.

   Start by noticing the visual aspects, the qualities of the picture: size, distance, brightness, distance, color, and so on, and then systematically vary each quality to see which produces a significant change in the way you feel about the experience. For example, if you send the picture further away does that alter how you feel about the memory? What if you change the size of the picture or put a border round it? What happens when you make black and white? Out of focus? (Use the list in Figure 4.2 to help you here.) Then find which sound cues make a difference. What happens when you change the voice qualities or tonalities? What if you change the speed, or vary the pitch?

Something in this cue image triggers your response of fearing blocking – it's already swishing your mind to a very unresourceful state. What you are going to do is utilize this same ability to swish yourself into a resourceful state by changing the image. Instead of *fear*, you can have that cue image generate *calm* or *courage*.

3. **Develop a desired outcome picture.**
   There are contexts in your life when you speak fluently.

   • When do you speak fluently? Re-access a movie of these occasions.
   • What would your self-image of being fluent in all contexts look, sound and feel like? You already know something about the qualities of the image which created blocking, so those should be absent in your movie of fluency.

   You are going to create an enhanced image of the fluent you, by amplifying the positive cues that let you know you are in a good state. As in step 2, adjust the qualities of this image so that you feel even better. One difference is that you are going to see this image *dissociated* – you can see yourself in it. Create a picture for the *new you* – the you that would see when you no longer have that blocking behavior.

   • Do you like this new picture? Do you find it compelling? Attractive?

   The fluency image should draw you toward it. Edit the image so that it becomes even more attractive. Add in the qualities of *confidence*, *assertiveness*, *power*, *kindness*, and so on, so that this picture compels you to move toward it.

4. **Link the two representations.**
   Beginning with the cue picture of the fear of blocking from step 2. Make it big and bright.

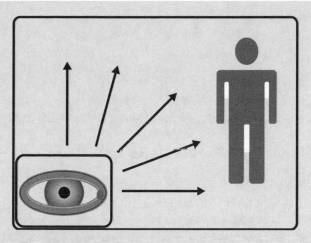

Figure 6.4: The Swish Pattern

Into the lower left corner of that picture put a small, dark image of the second picture from step 3. This is the dissociated image of the new you with the qualities of fluency (See Figure 6.4).

You are fully associated in the first picture and dissociated in the second. You do not need to see this second picture in detail; you just need to know it's there in the lower corner.

5. **Swish the pictures.**
Now you are going to do two things simultaneously. One is to take the large bright picture of you fearing blocking and quickly make it small and dark. You can do this by sending it off into the far distance, so that it becomes no more than a dot. At the same time, make the small dark image of the fluent you large and bright so that it fills the space vacated by the previous image. Do this very quickly. Remember, the mind learns fast.

As the clinician, you can assist the PWS in swishing the images by making a soft swishing sound as they do it.

Let the picture of the new fluent you for whom blocking is no problem swish in and completely cover the screen of your mind. Juice it up so that it is there in 3-D and coded in the ways that your mind knows is real, compelling, and attractive. You do all of this very quickly, in a fraction of a second.

When you have done that, clear the screen. Either close your eyes and blank out the screen, or open your eyes and look around.

6. **Swish five times.**
Now, do it again. Go back to the linked pictures and repeat this process. Clear your mental screen after each swish.

Do this procedure at least five times.

7. **Test.**
The last step is to test that this has worked. Think back to that cue picture that used to set you off and trigger that state of fearing blocking. Notice what happens now as you do that.

As you think about that old trigger, does your mind now immediately go to the new picture of the you for whom fluency is the norm? If so, that means you're done. You have successfully swished your mind so that it now has the new link. If not, then you need more practice.

Variations

There are other ways of exchanging the images.

• Make the cue picture of the fear of blocking associated and big and bright right in front of you. (Be in the picture. Do not see yourself, just see the other events as if there.)

• Place a small, dark and dissociated picture of the "you" for whom blocking is no problem out on the horizon. (In the resourceful picture, see yourself having the resource.)

• Swish the images by zooming the cue picture out to the horizon, making it smaller and darker until it becomes a tiny black dot. At the same time, zoom in the image of fluency, making it bigger and brighter so that it completely fills up the space where the old image was. Make it 3-D and very appealing.

- Do this really fast. Repeat five or six times faster and faster and test.

- Another way is to imagine putting the desired image out in front of you on a piece of elastic. Imagine a strong elastic band around your head, and the desired image, small and neat, as the pellet in a catapult. Hold that image in the elastic and pull the elastic back (actually use your arm as you imagine doing this). When it is at its farthest reach, when you are ready, suddenly let go so that the new image slams into your forehead. Feel the impact as this image replaces what was there before!

"Yes" and "No"

This section is about regaining your power by saying Yes to fluency and No to disfluency. This variation of the Swish Pattern uses verbal swishes. Actually all of the patterns involve saying No to what you don't want and Yes to what you do want – which in itself is a swishing process. However, no technique works for everyone all the time so your toolbox for change needs several tools.

Congruent "Yes" and "No"

Can you hold a thought in your mind that you don't believe? Sure you can. I can hold the thought that the sun will come up in the west in the morning – but I don't believe it. I can hold a thought that when I die I will be worth a billion dollars but I sure don't believe it. Well, what distinguishes a thought from a belief? Actually, it is quite simple. A belief is a thought that you have said Yes to

When you congruently say Yes to a thought, you associate into that thought. The effect of saying Yes is to put you *inside* the thought, as it were, to *accept* it instead of just thinking about whatever it was. The more often you say Yes to a thought, the more real it becomes, the more it features in your model of the world. A belief which is integrated into your system of meaning influences your thinking and behavior. For example, if you say Yes to the belief that you can be fluent in all contexts, then you get on and do it. If it just remains a thought – which is often the case with much that you read in Self-Help books – you are not committed to *doing* anything. By committing yourself, by saying Yes, you make it real and become sufficiently motivated to take action to change the behavior.

The reverse is also true. You can change your behavior, become uncertain, unmotivated by converting a belief back into a thought by saying No to it. Again, this may take some repetition. But guess what? It works! I have had several people state, "It can't be that simple!" Well, yes, it is that simple. A key aspect of all behavior change is saying No to what you don't want and saying Yes to what you do want. If you can congruently accept or reject a belief – with the whole of your body, mind, and spirit – you have the means to change your behavior at will.

How many beliefs did you once hold that you no longer subscribe to? I use to believe that Santa Claus came down the chimney, but I don't believe that anymore. Gradually and painfully I gathered enough evidence to say No to that belief. Now note that I said, "I gathered enough evidence." I changed that belief into a thought by saying No to it in stages. I started to become uncertain, and this was reinforced by my peers and by my parents who sort of admitted that they had been responsible for all the presents. But hey, you can give yourself a huge present by saying Yes to fluency, and No to stuttering and blocking. Are there any reasons for not doing this?

Exercise 6.3: The *No to Yes* Pattern

Use this process for changing your current limiting beliefs about stuttering and blocking. This technique provides a quick and effective way of removing any limiting beliefs and of installing empowering beliefs which support your commitment to success in fluency. This pattern for decommissioning old programs is one of the PWS's favorites.

Preparation: Check the ecology for this pattern before you use the process. You need to ensure that you have a top-notch belief that you want to confirm as being true for you.

What enhancing and empowering beliefs would you really like to have running that would allow you to say a great big "No" to those limiting beliefs around blocking and stuttering? Which of those beliefs stands in your way the most?

- Have you had enough of it? Or do you need more pain?
- When you no longer have that belief, is that OK with all parts of you?
- Will It be OK to not have that belief in your family life, work life and social life?

What empowering belief would you like to have in its place?

- What could you say a great big "Yes" to instead having that old limiting belief?"
- As you think about having that new belief, is it OK with all parts of you?
- Will it be OK to have that new belief in your family life, work life and social life?

For example:

- I will say "No" to believing that *I am a failure* because I block and stutter.
- I will say "Yes" to believing that *I am innately a person of worth.*

Overview

1. Get a No – Access a good strong *No!*
2. Say "No!" to the limiting belief
3. Access a strong and robust *Yes!*
4. Say "Yes!" to the enhancing belief.
5. YES the "Yes!" repeatedly and put into the future.

1. **Get a No – Access a good strong No!**
   Think of something that you can say "No!" to, with every fiber of your body, in a way that is fully congruent. For example: Would you push a little child in front of a speeding bus, just for the fun of it? Would you eat a bowl of disgusting filth?

   Say that "No!" repeatedly until you can notice how you image that. Take a mental snapshot of it.

147

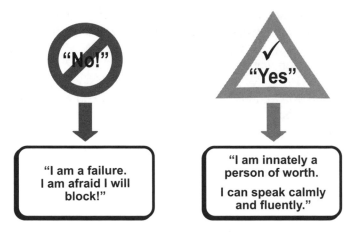

Figure 6.5: "No" to "Yes"

Anchor your No! with a with a physical gestures. Feel the No in your body; hear your voice saying "No!"

2. **Say "No!" the limiting belief.**
Feel all of this powerful "No!" fully as you think about that stupid, useless, limiting belief (for example: "I am afraid I will block").

And you can keep on saying "No!" to that limiting belief until you begin to feel that it no longer has any power to run your programs, or that it has no more room in your presence or in your mind.

And how many more times, with what voice, tone, gesturing, do you need to totally disconfirm that old belief so that you know deep inside that it will no longer control your behavior?

3. **Access a strong and robust Yes!**
Think about something that every fiber of your being says "Yes!" to without any question or doubt. (For example: "I love my children". It doesn't matter where you get the Yes so long as it is a powerful Yes!)

Notice the qualities of your Yes! and amplify those qualities to make this Yes! even more positive.

Anchor your Yes! with a different physical gesture. Feel the Yes! in your body. Hear your voice saying "Yes!"

4. **Say "Yes!" to the enhancing belief.**
    And feeling that "Yes!" even more fully, utter it repeatedly to that empowering belief that you want. For example, "I speak calmly and fluently."

    Do you want this? "Yes!" Really?

    How many more times do you need to say "Yes!" right now, in order to feel that you have fully welcomed it into your presence?

5. **YES the "Yes!" repeatedly and put into the future.**
    This is only an exercise. Do you want to keep this!
    You really want this?
    Would this improve your life?
    Would it be valuable to you?

The Drop Down Through pattern

From the many ways of creating change, those patterns which I have found work well with PWS are the ones included in this book. Although they address the specific issue of blocking and stuttering, they can easily be adapted for wide general usage. With so many to choose from, how do you decide which to use? Which is going to work most efficiently for the particular person you are with right now? That is a difficult question to answer because it depends on that person in front of you: how does change happen for them; how motivated are they to change? Do they really want to change; are they ready to let go of the benefits their old behavior provided? Your choice also depends on how well you understand their model of the world, because that affects your way of intervening in it.

However, if I were to suggest one pattern that works extremely effectively with people who block, it would be the *Drop Down Through* pattern. Indeed, in all the time I have been using it – over eight years – I have had more success with it than with any other single pattern. I am indebted to Tad James (James, 1987–1994) for introducing me to this pattern. This pattern can be used with any cognitive/emotional problem in which the person experiences a negative feeling. Over the years, I have made some modifications to the original (I have added step 5), but it remains simple in structure.

Essentially the person re-experiences their limiting emotional state and then mentally drops down through a number of layers which lie beneath it. With emotions, the metaphor of going down through layers works best. As they encounter each new layer, the person brings to conscious awareness the previously unconscious frames of mind that were supporting the layers above. The Drop Down Through Pattern provides a quick way to uncover the systemic nature of the problem, and the PWS will find it easy to apply the appropriate resources for resolving the issue and healing themselves.

CASE STUDY 10

Before I explain the pattern in detail, here is a transcript of a dialogue I had with a client. At a very early age Joe had witnessed the divorce of his parents. Joe began stuttering as a small child before his parents divorced. One parent later remarried, but the step-parent was extremely jealous of Joe and indeed seemed to work hard at showing favoritism towards his own children, and would shame Joe at every opportunity. This went on for years. During these critical years, Joe's blocking grew worse and worse. He had wrapped his shame-based personality around his blocking. My dialogue with Joe went like this:

"Joe, so you felt a lot of shame from the way your step-dad treated you?"

"Yes."

"Where do you feel this shame in your body?"

"It is in my chest."

"Now, Joe, I want you to just imagine yourself dropping down through that shame in your chest. And as you drop down through that, what thought or feeling is underneath that?"

"Anger. There is one mad little boy there."

"That is great. Now, Joe, I want you to just imagine yourself dropping down through that anger. And as you drop down through that, what thought or feeling is underneath that anger?"

"More anger."

"That is great. Now, Joe, I want you to just imagine yourself dropping down through that more anger. And as you drop down through that, what thought or feeling is underneath that?"

"Sadness."

"Now I want you to just imagine yourself dropping down through that sadness. And as you drop down through that, what thought or feeling is underneath the sadness?"

"Never a free kid."

"Good Joe. Now just continue dropping down through that never being a free kid and what is underneath that?"

"Nervous. Timid. I was always nervous and timid as a kid."

"And underneath being a nervous and timid kid, what is underneath that?"

"Scared. He scared the shit out of me!"

"You are doing really well, Joe. Just drop down through that and what thought or feeling is underneath that thought of your step-dad scaring the shit out of you?"

"Sadness."

"And continuing on down, what thought or feeling is underneath the sadness?"

"Agitation."

"Good Joe. And what is underneath agitation?"

Joe pauses.

"Nothing. There is nothing else there."

"That is great Joe. Now just imagine yourself opening up that nothingness and imagine yourself dropping down through that and what is out the other side of that nothingness?"

"I don't care. There is the thought that I don't care about all that stuff."

"Wow! Joe. That is fantastic. Now, just drop down through the 'I don't care' and what thought or feeling is underneath 'I don't care'?"

"Strength. I feel strength."

"Great. And what is underneath strength?

"There is that part of me that I mentioned earlier to you that loves me. It is the part that I sense of my loving myself."

"Yes, you mentioned to me earlier that you always sense that you had a part of you that truly loved yourself and that you just had trouble accessing it. Well, we know where it is, don't we? And what is there underneath the part that loves you?"

"Resilience. I see the sun. I have a picture of the sun and it is warm and calm. I feel safe here."

"I am wondering Joe, what does this state of being in the sun mean to you?"

"It is God. He is here."

(Joe was speaking in complete fluency and indeed had been since he dropped down through and out the other side of the nothingness. Most people who block do speak fluently once they reach this point.)

"That is great Joe. Now what we want to do is to really get this state anchored in so you can *fly there* anytime you want to."

(Those who have come to master their blocking have been able to get this state so locked in and so familiar that they can just go there at will. It usually takes some weeks of practicing but you will get there. So just note what you see, hear and feel and put a word or a phrase to it as a trigger so that you can recall this state anytime you want to. If you fear a block coming on, you can just think of or see the sun and go there.)

"Now, Joe you are doing really well. Being there now in the sun light feeling that warmth; having that sense of strength, resilience, safety and calm I want you to take that state and apply it to the shame from your step dad. How does this transform and enrich shame?"

"It evaporates it."

"And once it is evaporated, what state takes its place?"

"Healthy. I feel healthy."

"That is great Joe. Now having the state of strength, resilience, safety and calm I want you to take that state and apply it to the anger. What happens to anger in the presence of strength, resilience, safety and calm?"

"It evaporates it. But I can still feel a little bit of it. I see one mad little boy."

"That is OK Joe. Now, if you take that picture of the mad little boy and move him inside the sunshine, what happens to him?"

"Oh, he is playing and doing what little boys should be doing. He is having fun."

"Fantastic. Now having the state of strength, resilience, safety and calm I want you to take that state and apply it to the sadness. What happens to sadness in the presence of strength, resilience, safety and calm?"

"It evaporates it. The sadness is gone. It is now joy."

I continued this same pattern of questioning Joe as Joe took his resource state and applied it to each of the negative frames one at a time. (Applying resources – meta-stating – is the additional step I added to the original Drop-Down Through Pattern.) Did this move Joe to complete fluency? No, but it sure provided an excellent piece for the total therapy. And now that Joe knows how to do the Drop Down Through Pattern, he can do it on himself. We continued to utilize this pattern throughout his therapy.

Exercise 6.4: The Drop-Down Through pattern

Overview

1. Identify the experience with the emotion that you want to transform.
2. Step into that experience, and re-experience the emotion to some degree.
3. Drop down through the experience until you reach "emptiness" "void" or "nothing".
4. Confirm the emptiness and then continue to drop-down through and move to the "other side" of emptiness.
5. Associate into your resource state (fifth position) and apply that resource state to each problem state.
6. Test.

1. **Identify the experience and emotion you want to transform.**
   - What do you feel just before you block?
   - What feelings/emotions are behind your blocking?
   - What emotions or experiences are there which undermine your success as a fluent speaker, and which you would like to eliminate?

2. **Step into that experience.**
   Being aware of a particular experience you would like to work on, associate fully into that experience. Be present in that memory, looking through your eyes, hearing what you heard and feeling what you felt then.
   - Where do you feel this emotion in your body?
   - What does it feel like?
   - On a scale of 1–10, how intensely are you experiencing this emotion?

- Good. Just be there with it for a moment, noticing ... noticing it fully ... knowing that it is just an emotion, and knowing that you are so much more than any emotion ...

3. **Drop down through the experience.**
   This may feel strange at first, but you do know what it feels like when you drop ... So feeling that feeling of dropping, just drop down through that experience until you find yourself underneath that feeling ...

   - What thought, feeling or emotion lies underneath that original emotion?
   - And now just imagine dropping down through [that feeling] (use the exact words the person gives you)
   - And what thought, feeling or emotion comes to you as you imagine yourself dropping down through [that one]?

   Repeat this dropping down through process until the person arrives at some version of "emptiness" (Figure 6.6). That is, they experience a lack of feelings, some kind of void or nothingness.

   Note: Not everyone experiences the void or nothingness. They drop straight down through the negative frames into the positive ones. Sometimes they may just pause briefly as they make the switch from negative to positive.

   Some people reach a point near or at the void where they say things such as, "That is it. There is nothing else" or "I am at the bottom. There is nothing else below. I can't go any further." This may be visual (some kind of barrier or floor) or kinesthetic (a feeling of impenetrability or resistance). If this happens, suggest that this is to be expected, and that all they have to do is to imagine opening up whatever is blocking them in any way at all (they can be very creative here) and simply drop down another level. For example, one client reached the bottom and said, "I am standing on a two inch thick steel plate." I invited the client to imagine taking a cutting torch and cutting through the steel plate and then drop on down through. That worked. Use your creativity to do whatever it takes to get down through and out the other side. It's a case of asking your mind to find a way to "just do it" rather than agonize about how hard it is. As they let go of their resistance they will drop down through that and out the other side.

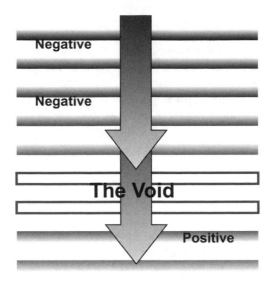

Figure 6.6: Dropping down through

4. **Confirm the emptiness and move down through to the "other side" of emptiness.**
   - Just experience that "nothingness" or "void" for a moment. Good.
   - Now let that nothingness open up and imagine yourself dropping through and out the other side of the nothingness.
   - What are you experiencing when you come out the other side of the nothingness? What or whom do you see? What resources are you aware of?

   Repeat this several times … to elicit further resource states.

   When you drop down through to the level of nothingness or the level where there is no meaning and from there you go through that "nothingness" you become able to access resource states. If you keep going you arrive at a fifth position point of view. For instance, if you ask a PWS, "What is behind your belief that other people think you are stupid if you stutter?" and keep asking them, "And what is behind that?" and so on, you will eventually elicit their fifth position beliefs. Whichever metaphorical direction you travel in, you eventually arrive at your "higher" frames of mind. You could say that every problem brings with it its own resource for healing. This is true for any problem for any person.

5. **Associate into your resource state (fifth position) and *apply* that resource state to each problem state.**
   - Apply each resource state to each problem state.
   - And when you feel X (resource state) about Y (problem state), how does that transform things?
   - And when you even more fully feel X – what other transformations occur?
   - Validate and consolidate: just stay right here in this X resource, and as you experience It fully, what happens to the first problem state (step 1)?

6. **Test.**
   - Let's see what now happens when you try – and I want you to really try – to get back the problem state that you started with.
   - When you try to do that, what happens? (There is a presupposition here that they cannot do this, at least to the same degree as before.)
   - Do you like this? Are you able to say Yes to validate the change?
   - Would you like to take this into your future – into all of your tomorrows and into all your relationships?

Conclusion

I am concluding with the Drop Down Through Pattern because it beautifully summarizes the ideas in this book. This pattern presupposes that blocking and stuttering are learned behaviors. The pattern elicits the unconscious meanings that keep the block in place. It then engages the mind in thinking in a different way, changing the PWS's point of view, and thereby changing the meaning of their experience. It also uses the meta-stating pattern – applying a positive, life-enhancing resource – for reframing those negative frames of mind which are triggered by all those old memories which hold the block in place long after it has ceased to provide a service to the PWS.

The ultimate goal of this pattern – as is the case with all the patterns in this book – is to lead the PWS to the point where they are no longer fixating on *how* they talk. Instead they are paying attention to the other person and engaging in mutually satisfying communication. The blocking and stuttering is no longer on their mind. When they reach that point, they have normal fluency.

Appendix A

Pioneers

John Harrison

I am not the first one to indicate that blocking has its roots in cognition (thinking). In the field of stuttering, John Harrison (1989, 2002) has provided a basic systems model describing six key variables or factors involved in stuttering. He calls this system, *The Stuttering Hexagon* (Figure A.1. See also Chapter 1):

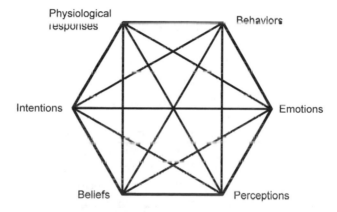

Figure A.1: The Stuttering Hexagon

The six factors are: *physiological responses, physical behaviors, emotions, perceptions, beliefs,* and *intentions*. Harrison points out that in a system every element is influenced by the other elements, positively or negatively (Harrison 1989: vi).

Harrison has also noted numerous other systemic factors about the stuttering hexagon:

- As a system, stuttering involves the entire person and is not just a speech problem.

- Once operating as a system, the hexagon "has a life of its own" (1989: 3).
- As a system, the stuttering system will develop default settings.

    "A permanent change in your speech will happen only when you alter the various default settings around the Stuttering Hexagon." (106)

- Change a critical factor in the system, and the entire system changes.

    Not everyone develops a blocking system. That emerges from a natural tendency for speech to stumble under stress. Harrison calls such stumbling in speech "bobulating". Harrison describes it as "... kind of a relaxed, stumbly disfluency that you hear when people are upset, embarrassed, confused or discombobulated. The person is able to talk but their emotions are causing them to trip all over themselves."

    Bobulating is effortless disfluency; it is not blocking because it often shows up when one is embarrassed, upset, confused or disoriented.

Harrison believes that to move from "bobulating" to blocking necessitates a certain way of perceiving speech and believing things about yourself and others. It invokes a specific sense of fear and apprehension, a certain attitude about how to cope and respond and this then coaches and trains the muscles involved in breathing to produce blocking.

For Harrison this means that there is a non-blocking mentality just as there is a blocking mentality. I agree totally. Notice in his Stuttering Hexagon how many of the six factors relate directly to the PWS's thinking and the interaction of thinking with the body:

1. Intentions – what the person desires.
2. Beliefs – what the person affirms as true for them.
3. Perception – how the person's model of reality reflects their experience.
4. Emotions – how the person feels about the experience.
5. Behaviors – how the person responds to their perceptions.

6. Physiological responses – the embodied consequences of their thinking.

Dave Elman

The hypnotist Dave Elman (1900–1967) was inspired by his father to take up hypnosis. Elman went on to train medical doctors and dentists. He describes the times doctors brought stutterers to the classes on hypnosis that he taught hoping that he could help them. He spoke of the pity he felt for these children and even more so the distress he felt when he met an adult who had a similar problem. Concerning stuttering he concluded, "There is no such thing as a congenital stutter. A stutter or stammer must be precipitate."

In the mid-twentieth century hypnosis was considered by many in the medical profession to be hocus pocus. However, Elman had a great understanding of cognition in addition to anatomy and physiology, and by limiting his trainings to doctors and dentists he successfully managed to make hypnosis more respectable. He knew that for hypnosis to work the cause of stuttering could not primarily be physical or inherited. He concluded:

> It is my firm belief that every stutter has a basic, investigable cause. Over the years, I have tried to get doctors to change their attitude towards stutterers and treat the *cause* rather than the *effect* ...
>
> Even a minor trauma can, like suggestion, be compounded by repetition. Every stutter has its beginning in a situation in which the victim reaches a point where he doesn't want to talk and yet is obliged to.

In other words, he firmly believed that blocking was caused by traumatic situations.

Carl H. Scott

Carl H. Scott, a California State licensed and ASHA-certified speech pathologist, suggests that blocking should not be treated just as a physical problem but as a cognitive problem. In working with people who block, he "considers the whole person and works toward a balance in mind, body and spirit." Scott has a three stage approach for therapy with people who block:

1. The first stage in this healing process is to guide the individual to identify the beliefs, attitudes, thoughts, feelings and behavior that may serve as obstacles in daily living and in accessing fluency.

2. The second stage is this therapeutic journey calls for initiating a healing process. This may involve working with his inner child, dialog or forgiveness.

3. The third stage of therapy is to guide the person who blocks into a healthy belief system with new and powerful positive thoughts and the ability to experience self acceptance and love. It also calls for manifesting changes in behavior.

Tim Mackesey

The speech pathologist and former stutterer, Tim Mackesey, writes about his experience using the tools that work most effectively in these cases:

> Neuro-Semantics and the NLP *Drop Down Through* Pattern offer great possibilities in the treatment of stuttering. Traditional speech therapy has centered around modifications at the behavioral level (i.e., breathing, easy onset of speech, light articulatory contacts, etc). The perceived stigma of stuttering and the overwhelming urge to "not stutter" often overpower behavioral level strategies. Periodic relapse after treatment is common. The missing Holy Grail from traditional speech therapy has been a consistent, swift, and thorough reframing strategy for meta-states to alleviate the pre-stutter phenomenon. Situation and word-specific anchors form along the timeline of stuttering development. As an NLP practitioner and person with a residual, mild stutter, I was game to explore the *Drop Down Through* process personally. I have experienced a significant increase in spontaneous fluency after just a few telephone consultations with Bob.

The *Drop Down Through* technique is explained in Chapter 6.

Systemic thinking

Current neuro-scientific thinking confirms our conjecture that the mind-body system works as a systemic whole and parts cannot be separated, and that as a consequence, emotions can and do find expression in particular areas of the body.

When a person has a panic attack, there are definitely physical symptoms. The bible for describing mental and emotional disorders used by those practitioners of counseling and psychiatry in the United States is *The American Psychiatric Association Diagnostic Criteria* better known as the *DSM-IV*. DSM-IV offers this description on diagnosing a panic attack:

> **A Panic Attack** is a discrete period in which there is the sudden onset of intense apprehension, fearfulness, or terror often associated with *feelings of impending doom*. During these attacks, symptoms such as *shortness of breath, palpitations, chest pain* or *discomfort, choking* or *smothering sensations* and fear of going "crazy" or losing control are present. [italics added]

I have put the psychosomatic symptoms in italics. If you were to move the expression of those emotions to those areas of the body which control speaking then you have blocking. The structure is the same; the expressions are different. Reframe or heal the emotions and the physical expression disappears.

Beyond Stammering: The McGuire Programme For Getting Good At The Sport of Speaking

The McGuire Program for people who stutter is one of the better known methodologies for gaining more fluency. It has wide acceptance and is used extensively. This program as well recognizes the psychological issues surrounding blocking and stuttering. In Part One "How to Get It" (McGuire, 2002: 7–8) the author lists the following objectives for their participants:

> *Physically:* the objective is to speak powerfully from the thorax by retraining your costal diaphragm.

Mentally: there are six objectives:

1. To understand the dynamics of stammering.
2. To counteract the tendency to "hold-back" and use avoidance mechanisms.
3. To deal with the fear through concentration and non-avoidance techniques.
4. To accept yourself as a recovering stammerer until you have proven yourself "a fluent speaker with occasional reminders of your past affliction".
5. To develop an assertive attitude to attack your remaining feared situations.
6. To understand the process of relapse and how to counteract it.

Note that in step 3 he addresses the ever present fear that stutterers live with. In my work I have discovered that the PWS demonstrates what is almost a universal fear of what others may think of them because they stutter. Objective 4 addresses the fundamental issue of self-esteem. I believe this is paramount and that is why this work has covered it thoroughly. Finally in Objective 5 McGuire points out the need for the PWS to become assertive – to exercise their own power rather than giving it away.

Summary

It is becoming increasingly recognized that blocking and stuttering are primarily learned behaviors – a view supported by Carl Scott, John Harrison, Dave Elman and a growing body of health professionals. John Harrison states that the problem is much more cognitive then physical. Other researchers agree with this conclusion. For example, the linguist Wendell Johnson, who wrote a series of books and articles on Stuttering between 1928 and 1972; the hypnotherapist Dave Elman, (Elman, 1964), the psychologist Dave McGuire and his colleagues (McGuire et al, 2002) also suggest that stuttering is a learned behavior.

Appendix B

A Case Study

by Linda Rounds
with Bob G. Bodenhamer

This case study first appeared in the National Stuttering Association's newsletter *Letting Go*.

Imagine with me, if you will, that it is tomorrow morning and like all other mornings you wake up to face another day as a person who stutters. You begin your normal morning routine that in all appearances resembles any non-stuttering persons morning routine. In fact the only difference in your routine and a non-stutters routine is what is occurring in your mind. While the person who does not stutter is worrying about what to wear and if they are having a bad hair day, you are scanning ahead in your mind at what speaking threats might be awaiting you. You immediately feel anxious and fearful and begin to plan out how you can avoid threatening situations. The day plays out as you expected ... you were able to avoid some situations, others you were not. By the time you arrive home at night you are emotionally drained and have expended all your energy trying to keep your stuttering problem at a minimum or at best, hidden all together. But what if on this particular evening when you arrive home something new happens and you are handed the emotional tools to immediately control the stuttering? Too good to be true? Another empty promise? Not so fast, it really happened.

I began stuttering at the age of five; by the age of seven I was proficient at stuttering. I was fully equipped with every emotion and belief necessary to be good at stuttering. I carried those emotions and beliefs with me everywhere I went, even as I proceeded into adulthood. During my childhood school years once a week, instead of being allowed to go outside to play at recess time, I was often whisked away to speech therapy. In high school my well-meaning teachers felt I would overcome stuttering by providing me ample speaking opportunities in front of the class. Then as a young adult I enlisted in the Army for four years to help pay for my college education. The Army recruiter promised that the Army could help me overcome stuttering, what he didn't tell me was that their technique was to scare the stuttering right out of me. None of these methods were very helpful.

When I was 19 years old I made the most meaningful decision of my life. No, I am not talking about marriage, although that is very meaningful. I am talking about the decision to become a Christian. From that point on my perspective of life and the world did a 180-degree turn. However, becoming a Christian did not end my stuttering and the disappointment I felt over God's seeming lack of concern about my speech problem was no small matter through the years. But I will revisit that issue a little further down.

Now, you would think that most people who stutter would avoid professions that require a lot of speaking. This is probably true, however, for some unknown reason, 12 years ago I was drawn to a profession that not only required a lot of speaking but also a lot of public speaking. In actuality, it is due to the dynamics of my profession that set me on a relentless path to overcome stuttering.

Previous treatment
Before I go on to how I moved from stuttering to stability, I think it is note worthy to mention that I have tried some of the more popular treatments for stuttering with minimal success. After becoming very disenchanted (and thousands of dollars poorer), I began doing research on my own to see if I could discover the key to unlocking the mystery behind my stuttering. You see, I have always been bothered by the theories that stuttering is caused by a physical defect in the speaking mechanism and/or brain. It made me feel dis-empowered, like my only hope was to wait until they invented a magic pill that would cure stuttering. It also did not take rocket science to figure out that my speech mechanisms were in good working order since even my most difficult words could be spoken fluently in certain situations. And then there was that ever-present anxiety that always preceded the stuttering. Hmmm, I wonder what would happen if there were no anxiety?

This is where the story gets really interesting. One day I was surfing around on the National Stuttering Association's website when I spotted the book *How to Conquer Your Fears of Speaking Before People* by John C. Harrison. I ordered the book and when it arrived I immediately began devouring its contents. The first part of the book talked about specific techniques that people who stutter could use to be an effective public speaker. While this portion of the book was good, it was the second portion that was like breathing a breath of fresh air.

The second part included John's feelings about stuttering which included an overall sense that if you are trying to solve a problem without making headway chances are that you are trying to solve the wrong problem. His book indicated that he felt many stuttering treatments are not inclusive enough to fully describe the full dynamics of what drives stuttering. Basically, that a paradigm shift in the way we view stuttering is needed.

In his book, John states:

> "If stuttering were simply a problem with the mechanics of speech, we'd stutter all the time, even when we were alone. Rather, it seems to be an interactive system involving a number of different components, only one of which is physical. It is the way these components interact that creates a self-reinforcing system."

John goes on to describe what he has termed *The Stuttering Hexagon*. The Hexagon is composed of six points that include: physical behaviors, emotions, perceptions, beliefs, intentions, and physiological responses. On the Hexagon every point is connected to every other point. Concerning all points being connected John states:

> "This means that each element is influenced, either positively or negatively, by what's happening at the other locations on the Stuttering Hexagon. In other words, your emotions will influence your behaviors, perceptions, beliefs, unconscious programs and physiological responses."

For the remainder of the second part of the book Harrison explains each of the six points on the Hexagon in detail and how they inter-relate with one another. If a person who stutters has previously been working on changing their debilitating beliefs and has been successful but still carries negative emotions from past childhood traumas or hurts those emotions will have a negative affect on the remaining points on the Hexagon and throw the entire system off leaving the person still vulnerable to stuttering. So each point must be effectively dealt with. He also contends that to make the stut-tering disappear you can't focus on *solving* it – you must focus on *dissolving* it. In other words, to remove the problem you must alter its structure.

John's Stuttering Hexagon was the most accurate description of the mystery behind stuttering that I had read to date. And the fact that after 25 or 30 years of stuttering he was able to defeat it himself, gave me the final boost that I needed to know that I too, could overcome stuttering.

As excellent as John's book was it was never intended to be a ther-apy program or provide techniques for becoming more fluent. So, at the end of the book I was left with the question, "How do I get all of the points on the Hexagon positively biased?" Little did I know that shortly I would discover the answer: Neuro-Semantics.

Throughout his book John recommends several other books, including *Awaken the Giant Within* by Anthony Robbins. 'That book was my first introduction to *Neuro-Linguistic Programming* (NLP). Eventually this book led me to *The User's Manual for the Brain*, which is a comprehensive manual covering the NLP Practitioner course and is written by Bob G. Bodenhamer, and L. Michael Hall, the co-founders of Neuro-Semantics (NS).

As I was reading the books on NLP I became very excited about the potential of these techniques being effective tools in getting the Stuttering Hexagon to be positively biased as it related to my inability to speak fluently. Practicing some of the techniques in *Awaken the Giant Within* proved to be mildly helpful. But I remained hopeful that this could ultimately be the mechanism that would throw me into speech stability. I felt that if I could just work with someone trained in Neuro-Linguistic Programming that they might be able to walk me through the techniques that would prove most effective for people who stutter.

My opportunity presented itself when midway through *The User's Manual for the Brain* the authors indicated a website address for Neuro-Semantics (www.neurosemantics.com). The next day I visited the sight and discovered that they provided private consultations. BINGO!!!!!! Because of my Christian beliefs I chose to email Bob Bodenhamer. I knew through reading his book that he held the same Christian values that I did so I felt an element of trust in contacting him. Later I discovered that L. Michael Hall, held the same beliefs also.

When I received an email back from Bob indicating his willingness to work with me I was ecstatic! He indicated that he indeed had limited experience with four or five clients who stuttered but had obtained successful outcome utilizing the skills of Neuro-Linguistic Programming (NLP) and Neuro-Semantics (NS). Bob also felt that he stood a real chance of helping me over the phone, which alleviated the necessity of me flying to North Carolina to meet with him. We set up the first phone consultation for the following Friday.

So the big question you may be asking is, "What are Neuro-Linguistic Programming (NLP) and Neuro-Semantics (NS)?" NLP is a model that helps you take charge of your own thinking by developing effective strategies and representing your experiences in an effective manner. Neuro-Semantics incorporates higher level "meanings" into the structure of subjectivity. Our "states" involve the primary level neuro-linguistic thoughts-and-feelings in response to something out there in the world. That defines a Primary State. A Meta-State involves more. It involves our thoughts-feeling about our thoughts, emotions, states, memories, imaginations, concepts, and so on. It involves our meta-responses to previous responses. (Fearing the fear of stuttering).

Bob sums up one of the major concepts of NLP/NS in his statement, "In NLP/NS we hold the belief that each person has all the resources that they need in order to "fix" any cognitive (thinking) based problem they may have."

I don't know about you but that is music to my ears.

It is important to understand that the person utilizes their own resources to bring about change. Everybody, regardless of his or her station in life, operates from a belief system. This belief system is what we utilize to determine our self-esteem, our personal limitations, our viewpoint on the meaning of life, how others view us, what we can and cannot accomplish in life, and every other judgment we make about ourselves, others and the world we live in. There are as many belief systems as there are people. In assisting individuals to overcome cognitive problems, Neuro-Semantics first attempts to discover the person's unique belief system and then utilizes it to bring about change.

With that being explained let me move on to tell you about our first phone session together and the day I was handed the emotional tools to immediately control stuttering.

The first tool was actually given to me by Bob through an email he sent me on the day I requested consultation with him. He had already determined that I held a strong Christian belief system and therefore he used that system to bring about change in how I perceived things relating to stuttering. He said, "… I do believe that there is a great chance of taking care of this through phone consultations and email. For what will happen when your fear, anxiety and/or phobia comes into the presence of God?" When I first read that email my initial response was shock. Then laughter as I immediately envisioned a picture of three teeny, tiny men called Fear, Anxiety, and Phobia shrinking back and cowering in the awesome presence of God. Bob had effectively used my belief in God to reframe my thoughts of fear, anxiety, and phobia by forcing them together knowing full well that my beliefs would not allow the two to reside together.

A note on resources

In NLP/NS we hold the belief that each person has the resources they need for their own healing. We also believe in utilizing each individual's resources. We do not judge the resources, we use them. This subject found her highest resources in her Christian faith. I have learned over the years that a person's religious beliefs usually provide very effective resources, and that when they are applied to the problem state, the person experiences healing. However, even those people who do not hold any religious beliefs already have sufficient and appropriate resources to overcome any cognitively-based problem they may have. It is the nature of every human being to have the potential for healing themselves.

The consultation

Then came the phone consultation. After a brief period of getting acquainted Bob zeroed in on the feeling of anxiety that was so familiar to me, and to so many other people who stutter. He utilized a technique called "The Drop Down Through Technique" (see Chapter 5) which had its foundation in the works of Alfred Korzybski in his classic work *Science and Sanity*. From that work Tad James of Advanced Neuro-Dynamics devised the current "Drop Down Through Technique" and later it was revised by Bob and Michael by adding additional resources to it from Neuro-Semantics. The technique is designed to address unconscious thoughts like those that drive stuttering. The following transcript is taken from the therapy notes of Bob Bodenhamer:

> In our first phone conversation I (Bob) associated the client into her anxiety which simply means I had her really feel the anxiety. She had a "heavy and tightening" feeling in her stomach, a feeling she described as "holding back." Now move that up to the muscles that control the vocal cords and you have stuttering.
>
> From her position of experiencing this "heavy and tightening" feeling in her stomach I asked her to drop down through that feeling. "What do you feel underneath that feeling?"
>
> "I feel fear. Fear is there!" (Note that here we have a thought of fear, which ties right into anxiety.)
>
> "Drop down through the fear. What do you feel under the fear?"
>
> "Nothing. I don't feel anything."

"Good. Now, just imagine yourself opening up the 'nothingness.' And drop down through and out the other side of the nothingness?"

"I see people. It is a little bit scary. They are watching me. They are expecting me to say something."

"Yes. And what does that mean to you?"

"Well, I have a sense of wanting to go away and hide."

"OK. That makes a lot of sense to someone who tends to stutter when she speaks to a group of people. Now, just drop down through that thought-feeling. What do you feel below that?"

"Ummh. I feel safe. I feel pretty safe now."

"You are doing really great now. That is good and it is going to get better. Now just drop down through the feeling of being safe and what or who is underneath that?"

"I feel contentment. I feel alone but safe."

"Now just drop down through that feeling of contentment and safety. What or whom do you feel below that?"

"Warmth. Total acceptance! I feel total acceptance. There is no judgment here. I see a yellow light."

"Great. Is the light really bright?"

"Yes, it is. It is very bright."

"Yes, I know it is very bright. And Who said, "He is the light of the world?"

"Jesus."

"That is right and He is there isn't He?"

"Yes, it is God. He is the Bright Light."

"Very good and just be right there with God in the presence of warmth and total acceptance. Now, what happens to the anxiety in the presence of God?"

"It is gone."

"What happens to the fear in the presence of God?"

"It is gone."

"What happens to the sense of wanting to go and hide in the presence of God?"

"It is gone."

"Yes, they are all gone, aren't they?"

"Yes, they are."

"And in the presence of God, what happens to stuttering?"

"It is gone."

"Yes, and being there in the presence of God, notice what you see, hear and feel. Put a word or a phrase to that state so that when you recall that word or phrase you will immediately go into the presence of God. And anytime you have a sense that you might stutter, just go into the presence of God and you will get totally control of the stuttering."

Bob utilized my beliefs in Jesus by having me "bring the negative thoughts into the presence of God" which forced me to apply my faith and belief in an all-powerful God where, to her, each of those thoughts can't possibly reside. After we had completed this technique Bob utilized The Trans-derivational Search technique by having me remember the first time I felt the anxiety related to stuttering. My first memory of feeling the anxiety was with my mom. From my experience, my mom was unhappy with my stuttering and as a child I could easily detect her dissatisfaction with my speaking ability. Bob reframed this memory which effectively removed the impact of those past perceptions.

The results

So the question is, "How did this work in the following days after the 45 minute call with Bob?" Well, I kept track. The following Monday and Tuesday at work I had nine occasions where anxiety set in. Eight of the nine times I used the technique Bob used during our consultation session, and the words flowed as smooth as butter. However, one time I encountered a block that just came out of nowhere: no warning, just Wham!

The progress was amazing but now I wanted to ensure that the surprise blocks would not happen any longer. So I scheduled another session with Bob for the following Wednesday evening. We spent an hour on the phone that evening working through an issue that I had no idea had buried its roots into the foundation of the stuttering. It had nothing to do with stuttering per se but everything to do with the anxiety behind the stuttering. The issue came up while Bob was trying to determine what specifically I was doing to trigger the speech block. I had indicated that my biggest challenge was speaking in front of groups as opposed to one on one conversation.

We uncovered various feelings associated with speaking before groups such as feeling outnumbered, out of control, vulnerable and exposed. Becoming fully conscience of those feelings caused only a minor amount of discomfort. However, the feelings behind those initial ones were not as easy to deal with. As Bob worked with me to discover the "other" thoughts they eventually came screaming to my conscience mind. My mind immediately began an internal war of "to tell" or "not to tell". After what seemed like a very inappropriate amount of hedging around in response to Bob's question, I came to the conclusion that if I ever wanted to be 100% free of stuttering I was going to have to step out on a limb and reveal what I have refused to discuss since my youth.

So what was this childhood thing that reinforced the stuttering? Well, like too many other children, while I was growing up I experienced some traumatic events. I knew I could skirt the issue, hang up, and continue having a certain level of problems in my speech *or* I could meet it head on and overcome the stuttering. The two issues had intertwined and the trauma reinforced the stuttering.

An important point to make is that one of the great things about Neuro-Semantics is that it is not necessary to discuss the specifics of a given situation. (Because our mind works more from structure than content, the NS Practitioner usually needs very little content to assist the client in resolving the issue. See my article "Seven Keys to Personal Change" and Michael's article "Why Introduce 'Meta-Levels' to Modeling" for more information about structural change.) I never had to reveal much more than just the high level aspects of the trauma. But I did have to be prepared to deal with the thoughts in my mind. That is not always easy. However, in terms of John Harrison's Stuttering Hexagon it had to be effectively "reframed" in order to get all the points on the hexagon positively biased. Those blocks which just came out of nowhere probably would never have gone away without effectively dealing with all of the issues behind the anxiety and fear.

So for the remainder of the session Bob utilized specific Neuro-Semantic techniques to help bring about desensitization of the memories relating to the childhood issues. By the end of the session we had discovered that while anger toward the events surrounding my childhood was very apparent what was even more significant was the anger I felt towards myself as a child. In essence I blamed myself for the events of the past. The session came to an end and we set up another appointment for the following week.

What is interesting is that after this session the speech blocks totally disappeared. The issue had not been completely resolved but apparently enough had been dealt with to cause the blocking to disappear. I still had the "thoughts" of being a stutterer and occasionally I would get the physical sense that I would stutter or block but I never did. In essence the physiological aspects were still present which Bob later explained was a result of the muscles still being neurologically programmed (another point on the Stuttering Hexagon). I am not sure but I would venture to say that the stuttering may have eventually returned if we had not taken the time to deal with the anger I felt toward myself as a child.

Before I move to the third and final session it would be good to mention that during the three weeks that I had been having phone consultations with Bob I was also reading *Games for Mastering Fear* (2002) written by Michael Hall with Bob Bodenhamer. While reading it I eventually came upon the Cartesian Logic model, which is for ensuring that the four logical possibilities of an outcome are considered: what would or wouldn't happen if you did or did not change. I answered the first three questions with relative ease but when it came to the final question "What *wouldn't* happen if you *did not* keep your stuttering?" it took me a moment to figure out what it was really asking, and I had a difficult time coming up with the answer. And then, suddenly, out of nowhere, the statement, "It wouldn't keep people away from me" came slamming into my conscious mind. I was stunned trying to figure out where that came from. It was an almost laughable statement to me because I have always enjoyed being surrounded by people. But just as quickly as the statement came to me I realized exactly what it meant.

Although people play a very important part in my life, I had learned early in life to keep most of my deepest thoughts and feelings private. Now I was remembering the many times people who have crossed my path had made comments on how "private" I was in sharing personal thoughts and feelings. Stuttering was a way to keep people I loved in my life but at a safe distance. I was happy to take care of them emotionally but I could never allow them to take care of me emotionally. This, I suppose, was a behavior that I learned early in my childhood. As I reflected back on this I could plainly see how it was a protection mechanism. When friends and family would start asking questions that I perceived as threatening I immediately would begin to block and stutter. This was a way to let them know that I was not willing to go there with them and it worked quite nicely. Nobody wanted to watch me struggle when I spoke so they usually dropped the subject. So there it was ... the primary benefit I was receiving by stuttering. [There is further discussion on this in chapter 3.e) Overcoming Resistance – Accepting the Notion of Loss (Secondary Gain)]

From there I was able to go back and evaluate the reason why I felt I needed to maintain so much privacy and also if it was something that was still a valid behavior to keep today. My conclusion was that as an adult I do not need to have the stuttering protect me any longer. I also have the ability to evaluate on a different basis what should be shared and what should be kept private. The rules of my childhood are no longer valid.

The last session
Now on to the final session. During this session, Bob and I directly dealt with that intense hatred. The session was the most difficult of the three. Bob had me go back and visit the little girl at age seven. He asked me to bring her up to God (See "How to Take a Hurt [Bitter Root] to Jesus" – www.neurosemantics.com/Christian/BitterRoot.htm) but initially I was unable to do so because I felt she did not deserve to be with him. In fact, I felt that God himself would not want her there with him. I knew in my head how ridiculous my thoughts were but my emotions were filled with dislike and contempt for the little girl. Eventually Bob was able to find a way to get me to bring the little girl to God but it remained unnatural and I despised her invading my relationship with God. Then we shifted gears. Now the focus was on how the little seven-year-old girl felt. My comment to Bob was that she was "madder than spit fire". When Bob asked what or whom she was mad at, the events of the past were certainly mentioned, but the real anger she was feeling was at the grown up me. Her anger was that I was blaming her and that I refused to get on with my life. She wanted me to quit placing so much emphasis on the events of the past and to simply start being the adult. Wow.

After 30 minutes Bob cut off the session to allow me time to process what had just occurred. That certainly was a major turning point. The next day I sent Bob the following email message:

> "... After we hung up I went in to work out (great time for thinking and processing information) I had a lot of thoughts running through my mind. Let me bore you with some of them."

I was thinking of my seven-year-old niece (good age, huh?). From the day she was born she owned my heart. I desperately loved her and silently vowed to do everything in my power to ensure that she would never experience a traumatic childhood. Then I came to realize that I did not have the power to completely protect her.

Even my sister and brother-in-law did not have full power to protect their own daughter. Then I came to realize that God did not
give me the power to completely protect her. He did not even give
my sister and brother-in-law full power to protect their own
daughter. So I determined to do what He did give me the power to
do ... to unconditionally love her no matter what happened, to be
her advocate throughout life, to encourage, and to help teach her
how to love God and other people. So then I began to wonder why
I am able to love my niece so deeply regardless of what happens to
her. If anything ever happened to her I would just want to hold her
tight until the pain went away. Seems to me there should be no difference between my seven-year-old niece and myself at age seven.

So then I see myself looking back 31 years at a seven-year-old girl
and I am shouting, "Pack your bags and get out of my life!" The
seven-year-old girl is looking forward 31 years and shouting,
"Grow up, you're the adult! The answer is not back here!" It
dawned on me that she is right. No matter how many times I
replay the tapes of the past I won't discover the answer from a
seven year old. The seven year old did the best she could with the
resources she had. There are no answers in her mind, she is only
seven. So I shout back down to her again, "Hold on, I'm coming
back there." Now the little girl is smiling. I, being 38 years old and
operating with a strong belief system, begin to move back toward
her. When I reach her, I welcome her in my arms and give her the
same love that I would give to my niece. An interesting thing happens then: we both look at the individual who was responsible for
the events of the past and we see something new ... the emptiness
within that person's soul. I whisper to the little girl, "It was never
about you". Then I move forward and visit that little girl at each
stage of trauma while she is growing up and I repeat the same
process.

Then another thought occurred to me. Continuing to live with the
mind of a seven-year-old traumatized girl is in direct violation of
all the values and beliefs I hold as an adult. Beliefs such as: Jesus
has come to set me free, I am saved by grace not by works, I am a
new creature in Christ, I do not fear those who can kill my body
but have no power to destroy my soul, and all the other wonderful Biblical truths that I hang my life on. And then there are your

words ringing in my ears as you quoted Paul, "When I was a child I thought as a child but now I put childish thinking behind me".

So right now I feel better about that seven-year-old girl. I don't know what tomorrow will bring but today I not only look like an adult but I think like one also."

My first phone conversation with Bob took place on January 18, 2002. The immediate results were amazing. My second phone conversation was January 23, 2002. I have not stuttered since that time. My third phone conversation was on January 30, 2002. I have loved that little seven year old ever since.

So I have to ask, "Was God really unconcerned with my speech problem for the past 32 years?" I am of the opinion that he was very concerned about the stuttering. In fact, I believe his concern went way beyond the stuttering to the heart of who I am. I am convinced he was more concerned with healing all of me not just a symptom of stuttering.

In closing, I would like to mention that for me Neuro-Semantics was a very effective tool in getting the remaining points on the Hexagon in a positive mode. Although I believe that Neuro-Semantics can assist a great majority of people who stutter, I equally believe that the quick results I received were due in part to the work I had been (unknowingly) doing through the years to get the points on the Hexagon positively biased. I have learned that the core root may be different for each individual but the symptoms (anxiety, fear, muscle tension in the vocal cords and stomach, etc.) and the outcome (stuttering) appear to be the same. If, as suspected, the emotions such as fear and anxiety lie behind the stuttering, then Neuro-Semantics provides the tools for alleviating these unconscious negative emotions. And by alleviating these negative emotions, we alleviate the stuttering.

Two month follow up – is it working long-term?
After I had completed the consultations with Bob, I knew there would be certain milestones that would determine how effective the treatment was on a long-term basis. Those milestones included being placed in the usual "high stress" situations that would normally result in stuttering. Some examples are serious one-on-one

conversation concerning uncomfortable topics, Management meetings, Company meetings, and several other speaking situations that I previously thought of as "threatening". Over the past two months I have been exposed to each of these "threatening" situations and spoke fluently through each milestone. The final milestone was met on March 21, 2002 when I was scheduled to give a presentation to the Board Members of the Company I work for. Now, prior to working with Bob, stuttering in this situation was a 100% certainty. However, even that meeting was unable to produce the stuttering again. I have tested my fluency in every situation that used to produce stuttering! And I am happy to report that it appears to be a long-term success.

The biggest difference between stuttering and fluency is that fluent individuals do not think about stuttering.

It has been over two years since this therapy with Linda. A couple months ago I asked her how she was doing. She replied, "The thought of stuttering has no place in my mind any more." Linda and a friend started a new business venture specializing in preparing food for dogs and other pets. She has received a great deal of media attention. And at the time of this writing she wrote, "My speech continues to be awesome. Two years ago I would never have been able to do these interviews with reporters. It still feels great to be free." Amazing, when the PWS doesn't consciously or unconsciously think about stuttering the chances of stuttering is greatly diminished. When the person is fluent there are no fears of stuttering. They just are not there. When they block and stutter, the thoughts and fears are always there. So the purpose of therapy with a PWS is to assist them in thinking differently about how they talk.

How to contact the author

The Institute of Neuro-Semantics®
www.masteringstuttering.com
bobbybodenhamer@yahoo.com
704-864-3585

About Bob G. Bodenhamer, DMin

Dr. Bodenhamer's undergraduate degree (BA) is from Appalachian State University in Boone, NC (1972). His major at Appalachian State University was Philosophy and Religion with a minor in Psychology. He received the Master of Divinity (1976) and the Doctor of Ministry Degrees (1978) from Southeastern Baptist Theological Seminary in Wake Forest, NC. The Master of Divinity Degree included training in Pastoral Care with both classroom and clinical work. Dr. Bodenhamer received one unit of Clinical Pastoral Education from Wake Medical Center in Raleigh, N. C. while working on his doctorate. His marriage to Linda now spans 39 years.

His NLP Practitioner's Certification comes from L.E.A.D.'s Consultants in Reynoldsburg, OH, Dr. Gene Rooney, Trainer. Dr. Bodenhamer's NLP Master Certification and Master Time Line Therapy™ Practitioner Certification came from Tad James, PhD of Advanced Neuro-Dynamics of Honolulu, HI. Additional training has been received from NLP conferences. Dr. Bodenhamer has approximately 1500 hours of formal NLP training. He teaches NLP in the Corporate/Community Education program at Gaston College. Dr. Bodenhamer received his certification as a Trainer of NLP from Tad James, PhD, Advance Neuro Dynamics, Honolulu, Hawaii and Wyatt Woodsmall, PhD of Advanced Behavioral Modeling, Inc., Arlington, VA.

As an International Master NLP Trainer, he offers both certified training for Practitioners and Master Practitioners of NLP. He serves as a training and therapy consultant for corporations and he has a private NLP Therapy practice. Dr. Bodenhamer has served four Southern Baptist churches as pastor. He is presently serving as pastor of a mission church called Christ Fellowship Community Church. His time in the pastorate spans 34 years. All of his pastorates have been in North Carolina.

He co-founded the Institute of Neuro-Semantics with L. Michael Hall, PhD.

He has co-authored eight books with Michael Hall:

- *Patterns For Renewing The Mind: Christian Communicating & Counseling Using NLP* (1996) with Michael Hall
- *Figuring Out People: Design Engineering With Meta-Programs* (1997) with Michael Hall.
- *Time Lining: Advance Time-Line Principles* (1998) with Michael Hall
- *Mind-Lines: Conversational Reframing, 4th Edition* (1998, 2002) with Michael Hall
- *The Structure of Excellence: Unmasking The Meta-Levels of "Submodalities"* (1999) with Michael Hall
- *The User's Manual for the Brain: The Complete Manual for Neuro-Linguistic Programming Practitioner Certification. Volume I* (1999) with Michael Hall
- *Hypnotic Language: Its Structure and Use* (2000) with John Burton
- *The Structure of Personality: Modeling "Personality"* (2001) With Michael Hall, Richard Bolstad and Margot Hamblett
- *Games for Mastering Fear* (2001) with Michael Hall
- *The User's Manual for the Brain: Mastering Systemic NLP Volume II* (2003) with Michael Hall

The Institute of Neuro-Semantics is approved by The National Board For Certified Counselors to offer continuing education activity for National Certified Counselors. We adhere to NBCC education guidelines – provider #5724.

Further information is available from the following webites:

www.masteringstuttering.com
www.neurosemantics.com
www.runyourownbrain.com
www.meta-coaching.org
www.equilibrio.com.au

Acknowledgments

L. Michael Hall, PhD
A very special thanks goes to Michael Hall for much of the mate
rial that I have used in this book. Many of the patterns have been
adapted from his work in Meta-States® and Neuro-Semantics®.

Peter Young
This work would not be in published format were it not for the
editing ability of Peter Young. I first met Peter when he assisted me
with *The User's Manual for the Brain, Volume 1*. From that work I
learned about his ability to organize and present information.
Peter has a tremendous ability to get to the essence of the subject
matter, and to explain ideas clearly. I am extremely indebted to
him and his expertise.

Linda C. Bodenhamer
This book, as with all my joint works with Michael Hall and John
Burton, would have been impossible had it not been for the loving
support from my wife, Linda Bodenhamer. She has labored many
years to provide us with our financial needs freeing me to devote
time to develop such works as this one. For the 39 years of constant
love, support and encouragement, I owe her a special debt of
gratitude.

Linda Rounds
Without question, this project would never have been initiated
were it not for the encouragement of Linda Rounds, one of my first
clients who had a blocking and stuttering problem. Her knowledge of the stuttering community and her willingness to share it
with me and to encourage me in this pursuit launched me on the
path of dedicating much effort to this work.

PWS

In addition to Linda Rounds, there are many other People Who Stuttered. Tim Mackesey, David Lock, John Harrison and others have encouraged me to continue my work and research in this field in order to bring healing and fluency to many who have no other hope.

To those who attend the *Mastering Blocking & Stuttering Workshops* I owe a special debt of gratitude; having many PWS in a learning environment provides the trainer with immense opportunities for valuable feedback. I must also thank the many people on the neurosemanticsofstuttering@yahoogroups.com email list from whom I have learned a great deal and whose comments and suggestions I have been able to incorporate into my practice.

To all these and the countless thousands who daily fight a battle of trying to communicate, that few people other than those who share disfluency can understand, I dedicate this work.

About Peter Young, the Editor of this book

Peter Young is a writer, editor, trainer, and an NLP Practitioner. Since 1993 he has been producing NLP training notes, editing and ghost-writing books, and writing articles on NLP which have been published in *Rapport* (in the UK) and in *Anchor Point* (in the US).

He previously worked with Bob Bodenhamer in revising the first volume of *The User's Manual for the Brain*.

He has written three books of his own:

- *Understanding NLP: Metaphors and Patterns of Change*, Carmarthen, Crown House Publishing. (2001)
- *Change Manager*, London, Hodder Headline. Part of the Q-Learning *Be your best ... and beyond* series. (2003)
- *Understanding NLP: Principles and Practice*, Carmarthen, Crown House Publishing (2004)

He is currently working on *Understanding NLP: Language and Change*. His website is: www.understandingnlp.com

Bibliography

American Psychiatric Association Diagnostic Criteria, from DSM-IV, 1994, American Psychiatric Association, Washington DC.

Atkinson, Marilyn, 1997, *The Grammar of God*, Unpublished Manuscript, Vancouver, BC.

Bodenhamer, Bob G. and Hall, L. Michael, 1999, *The User's Manual for the Brain: The Complete Manual for Neuro-Linguistic Programming Practitioner Certification, Volume I*, Crown House Publishing Ltd, Carmarthen, UK.

Burns, David D., 1989, *The Feeling Good Handbook*, William Morrow and Company, Inc., New York.

Elman, Dave, 1964, *Hypnotherapy*, Westwood Publishing Co., Glendale, CA.

Ellis, Albert and Harper, Robert A., 1976, *A New Guide to Rational Living*, Prentice-Hall, Inc., Englewood Cliffs, NJ.

Hall, L. Michael, 1996, 2000, *Accessing Personal Genius Training Manual*, Neuro-Semantics Publications, Grand Junction, CO.

Hall, L. Michael, 2001–2002, The Neuro-Semantics of a Meta-Narrative Frame, in *The Meta-NLP Master Practitioner Training Manual*, Neuro-Semantics Publications, Grand Junction, CO.

Hall, L. Michael and Bodenhamer, Bob G., 2001, *Games for Mastering Fear: How to Play the Game of Life with a Calm Confidence*, Institute of Neuro-Semantics Publications, Grand Junction, CO.

Hall, L Michael and Bodenhamer, Bob G., 2001, *Mind Lines: Lines for Changing Minds*, Crown House Publishing Ltd, Carmarthen, UK.

Harrison, John C., 1989, 2004, "Anatomy of a block", part of a larger article entitled "The Power of Observation". In *How to Conquer Your Fears of Speaking Before People*, 10th Edition, National Stuttering Association, New York. The URL for the article is
www.mnsu.edu/dept/comdis/kuster/Infostuttering/Harrison/observation.html
www.stutternomore.com/Articles%20Primary/Anatomy_of_Block.htm
www.yeoyeogwan.org/english/board/stutter_pds/

James, Tad, 1987–1994, Course Notes for Master Time Line Therapy® Practitioner Training, Advanced Neuro Dynamics Inc.

Korzybski, Alfred, 1941, 1994, *Science and Sanity: An Introduction to Non-Aristotelian Systems and General Semantics*. (4th Ed & 5th Ed), Lakeville, CN: International Non-Aristotelian Library Publishing Co.

Lederer, Debra with Hall, L. Michael, 1999, *Instant Relaxation: How to Reduce Stress At Work, at Home And In Your Daily Life*, Crown House Publishing Ltd, Carmarthen, UK.

McGuire, Dave, 2002, *Beyond Stammering: The McGuire Programme for Getting Good at the Sport of Speaking*, Souvenir Press, Ltd., London.

Robbins, Anthony, 1992, 2001, *Awaken the Giant Within: How to Take Immediate Control of Your Mental, Emotional, Physical and Financial Life*, Simon & Schuster, Pocket Books, New York.

Scott, Carl H., October 1997, The mind-body-spirit therapeutic model for people who stutter. In *Letting Go* the Newsletter of the National Stuttering Association, Anaheim Hills, CA.

Seligman, Martin P., 1975, *Learned Helplessness: On Depression, Development, and Death*, Freeman, San Francisco.

Seligman, Martin P., 1990, *Learned Optimism*, Alfred A. Knopf, New York.

Young, Peter, 2004, *Understanding NLP: Principles and Practice*, Crown House Publishing Ltd, Carmarthen, UK.

Index